CHOOSING WHOLENESS OVER GOODNESS

CHOOSING WHOLENESS OVER GOODNESS

A PROCESS FOR RECLAIMING YOUR FULL SELF

THE OFFICIAL WORKBOOK COMPANION TO THE
NEW YORK TIMES BESTSELLER *ON OUR BEST BEHAVIOR*

ELISE LOEHNEN AND COURTNEY SMITH

THE DIAL PRESS | NEW YORK

The Dial Press
An imprint of Random House
A division of Penguin Random House LLC
1745 Broadway, New York, NY 10019
randomhousebooks.com
penguinrandomhouse.com

A Dial Press Trade Paperback Original

Library of Congress Cataloging-in-Publication Data
Names: Loehnen, Elise author | Smith, Courtney (Management consultant) author
Title: Choosing wholeness over goodness / Elise Loehnen & Courtney Smith.
Description: New York, NY: The Dial Press, [2025] | "A Dial Press Trade Paperback Original." |
Includes bibliographical references.
Identifiers: LCCN 2024061563 (print) | LCCN 2024061564 (ebook) | ISBN 9780593736876 trade paperback |
ISBN 9780593736890 ebook
Subjects: LCSH: Self-realization | Self-actualization (Psychology) | Deadly sins | Enneagram
Classification: LCC BF637.S4 L64 2025 (print) | LCC BF637.S4 (ebook) | DDC 158.1—dc23/eng/20250317
LC record available at https://lccn.loc.gov/2024061563
LC ebook record available at https://lccn.loc.gov/2024061564

Printed in the United States of America on acid-free paper

2nd Printing

BOOK TEAM: Production editor: Robert Siek • Managing editor: Rebecca Berlant • Production manager: Sandra Sjursen • Proofreaders: Muriel Jorgensen, Robin Slutzky, and Ying Gao

Book design by Jo Anne Metsch

The authorized representative in the EU for product safety and compliance is Penguin Random House Ireland, Morrison Chambers, 32 Nassau Street, Dublin D02 YH68, Ireland.
https://eu-contact.penguin.ie

To our children:
Maisie, Angus, Maude, Max, and Sam.
May we release our stories so you can write new ones.

I'd rather be whole than good.

CARL JUNG

Contents

CHOOSING WHOLENESS OVER GOODNESS

Introduction: Influenced

IS THERE A TRUER VERSION OF
YOU HIDING IN THERE?

When I wrote *On Our Best Behavior,* I wanted to pull apart the cultural programming that was running my life: specifically, the impulse I felt inside compelling me to be a *good woman,* the cattle prod pushing me to actually perform this goodness in the world. *What is this?* I wondered. *And where did this come from?* And more pointedly: *Why am I so terrified to give up this act?*

As I began my research, I knew I was working with a core premise: In our persistently patriarchal culture, women are conditioned for goodness, just as men are conditioned for power. To deviate from these edicts—for a woman to be perceived as "bad," for a man to be perceived as "weak" or "feminine"—is a type of social death. If we want something different for both women and men, we need to change these constructs. But we cannot do this until we come to understand how they constrain our lives.

Being a "good" woman, in a culturally sanctioned and adjudicated way, feels like the only real path to safety in our society. Reputational harm for women is dangerous, if not deadly: All you have to say is that a woman is *bad,* an unreliable friend, a cold mother, a toxic co-worker or boss, and she's done. Women will disappear themselves when these assaults on their goodness come: Cue every celebrity takedown, the removal of female founders, and so on. Our culture is a graveyard of women's reputations, and we are our own gravediggers. What's particularly pernicious is that women are trained to police not only ourselves but each other. Meanwhile, men can pretty much do *anything* that's grievous and harmful, so long as we perceive them as powerful.

You might scream, "I don't believe this" or "I don't choose this," but this is a (current) endemic reality in our Western society. I wish we could hit the "Unsubscribe" button or send this message straight to a spam folder with a single click, but that's not how our culture works. As I wrote in *On Our Best Behavior:*

> Culture is contagious: We pass it on to each other like a virus. It permeates everything. No one wholly invents themselves. Culture is whispered into us, transmitted through almost every interaction. "Nature" and "culture" are conflated and debated—the question of whether culture drives behavior or behavior creates culture will never be answered. What is apparent, though, is how twisted many of us feel, like a snake eating its own tail: What's me, versus the me I think I'm supposed to be?

By *culture* and *nature* I simply mean that we've been told stories as old as time about what a good woman is (hint: she hangs out in caves, nursing and tending to her young, waiting for her valiant man to return from a hunt or fight so she can reward him with sex), and we're convinced this is some version of our destiny—that to do something other than what our "nature" dictates is deviant. But this is actually a cultural story: Women were hunters too. Men have been caregivers since the dawn of time. It's our culture that dictates narrow bands of behavior. We may think we can opt out by ignoring these ideas, but it's not that simple.

Can you relate to any of this? A good woman is never tired. A good woman doesn't really want anything for herself; in fact she's happy to subjugate everything she wants to other people's needs. Speaking of needs, a good woman needs no attention, affirmation, or praise. A good woman has no appetite; in fact she has unswerving discipline for keeping her body small, under control, and compliant. A good woman doesn't talk about money (it's base!) and keeps the general economy humming and her own budget tightly constrained. A good woman is desirable but never desiring, sexy but not sexual. And a good woman is never upset—furious or depressed—about any of this.

This paragraph upsets me—in part, because I can recognize that despite doing the work to disentangle myself from these stories for many years, I'm still susceptible to them. They're tricky, particularly the idea that a good woman should subjugate her wants to other people's needs. To pursue what you want for yourself feels selfish, specifically in a culture that mandates that women should actually be selfless. Courtney and I are here to offer that there's a middle path—a way to prioritize self-expression *and* relationship simultaneously.

On Our Best Behavior explores why and how these rules about women and goodness came *to be.* This workbook will help you figure out what *to do.* It reveals how you can choose something else instead. We outline a process that begins by identifying the stories that are running your life, stories so closely held they've actually become your unconscious beliefs. As we tease these out in the following pages, you will choose *new* stories and beliefs that do not impinge on your ability to be yourself. The original word for sin—*hamartia*—means "to miss the mark": Our very human instincts, appetites, and desires are GPS points. When we get rigid about our stories and about who we should or should not be, we lose our ability to attend to this internal radar.

You can't shift the world alone. Too often, we're fed the lie that all problems are personal and that working on ourselves is enough—and that if it's not enough, there's something wrong with us. But changing culture is collective work, not individual work—even though it begins with ourselves. This workbook is about identifying what's running us, *all of us,* and helping each other become free. As you do this work, help a friend do it too so that you model your freedom for each other and support each other on a path to wholeness—a wholeness that includes *every part* of you.

After I published *On Our Best Behavior,* a good friend and Jungian psychologist commented that I had written a book about the cultural shadow of femininity. I had named everything that we've been conditioned to label as "bad" and thus disown—our appetites, our need for recognition and rest, our desire to say what we really want, and feel, and think. These natural human urges don't go "elsewhere" when we disavow them: We simply repress and suppress them in our bodies, and then ultimately project them onto other people (see the "Envy" chapter in *On Our Best Behavior*).

The poet Robert Bly offers a handy metaphor for this in *A Little Book on the Human Shadow,* as he likens our shadow to a trash bag that we haul around: "We spend our life until we're twenty deciding which parts of ourselves to put in the bag, and we spend the rest of our lives trying to get them out again." I had to laugh because not only was my friend's observation true—*On Our Best Behavior* is about the cultural shadow of femininity—but as an obsessed Carl Jung freak who works with a Jungian therapist, I had failed to see what I was up to. While I kept filling my Hefty until I was forty, I had just done two years of shadow work while writing the book, extracting all the parts of myself that I had denied. This work continues to this day.

As I wrote *On Our Best Behavior,* people often asked me if the book was about being *really bad* as an antidote—you know, was I going to spend a year pursuing all the sins, like sleeping with strangers, eating my way through the county's myriad buffets, and telling off strangers in the security line at LAX. "Not quite," I would reply, often to looks of disappointment. "It's a book about balance, about letting all our very human appetites and impulses come up so that we can reconcile them rather than pretending that they don't exist." *On Our Best Behavior* is about swapping out the pursuit of "goodness" and its veneer of perfection for the pursuit of wholeness instead—a wholeness that's large enough to contain every single part of us. I recognize that it can be terrifying for women to give up the label of goodness: "Who am I if I'm not a good mother?" Or "I don't know who I would be if I weren't a good citizen, an activist, someone who stands up for what's right." We're not asking you to give up goodness wholesale; we're asking you to replace the rigidity with which you hold this pursuit of perfection and its dialed-up behavioral code with something flexible and human instead. We are asking you to relax into the recognition and understanding that the depth and texture of your character and humanity come from your shadowy parts too. Let them in. It takes an awful lot of energy to stuff those parts away and keep that trash bag closed as you haul it through your days. Meanwhile, that trash bag is full of *gold,* should you dare to look.

With wholeness, nothing is excluded and everything belongs, even the parts of ourselves that we've been conditioned to believe are unsavory: They help us fill in the image of who we are. The other beautiful quality of wholeness is that while *it* is complete, we are not—life is an ongoing practice of reclaiming and realizing all these various parts of ourselves. It is a process of constant discovery and change. We get stuck only when we are mired in unconscious stories and social constructions, ideas that keep us fixed in place about who we are and how we need to be. Jungian therapist Robert Johnson writes about the question of wholeness quite simply in *Owning Your Own Shadow*: "Generally, the first half of life is devoted to the cultural process—gaining one's skills, raising a family, disciplining one's self in a hundred different ways; the second half of life is devoted to restoring the wholeness (making holy) of life. One might complain that this is a senseless round trip except that the wholeness at the end is conscious while it was unconscious and childlike at the beginning." It is our greatest hope that these pages get you moving once again, ready to commit to new and larger stories that not only include all the parts of you but feel consciously chosen instead.

MEET COURTNEY

You know those people who feel like past-life connections, whose lives so parallel your own it's beyond synchronicity? That's Courtney. Courtney is my kind of nerd: She was a math/economics major at Wake Forest and earned a JD at Yale and a master's in public health at NYU. After a long career as a consultant at McKinsey and elsewhere, Courtney took a left turn into the mystical world of the Enneagram, studying for years with renowned expert Russ Hudson. She then became a coach, relying on a diverse range of trainings alongside Enneagram: the Conscious Leadership Group, Byron Katie, Gay and Katie Hendricks, and so on. Like me, Courtney is a lifelong student who reads voraciously. In fact, if our libraries were a Venn diagram, they'd be a perfect circle. If there's a worthy modality, Courtney has likely trained in it.

One of the biggest synchronicities between my work and Courtney's is that the Seven Deadly Sins (the "punch card of goodness" that forms the superstructure of *On Our Best Behavior* and this workbook) I've studied and the Enneagram she's studied share a father: Evagrius Ponticus, an ascetic monk who lived in the Egyptian desert in the fourth century and wrote down "Eight Demonic Thoughts" and what to do about them. *Demon* had a very different definition then than it does now—this wasn't a fire-breathing devil but a demon that would distract or disturb you and keep you out of prayer. Ponticus's list included sadness, which was dropped when Pope Gregory I rebranded these "Demonic Thoughts" as the Seven Cardinal Vices and assigned them all to Mary Magdalene (speaking of stories with long teeth, you can find this history in *On Our Best Behavior*).

Just as my study of the Seven Deadly Sins informed my book and helped me to grow as a thinker, researcher, and cultural commentator, Courtney's study of the Enneagram shaped her understanding of personality development, internal dynamics, and how to help people change and evolve. I've been coached by Courtney (both individually and in group) and I've watched her coach others—it is a magical and moving experience, and I'm excited for you all to experience her genius in these pages.

In the spring of 2024, Courtney and I began co-leading retreats where we took groups of women through an experience that revealed the unconscious commitments they had made to certain stories—stories about how they needed to behave to be the women they believed they needed to be. These were stories about how they showed up with their families, partners, and friends; how they performed at work; and how they presented themselves to the wider world.

On the pages of this workbook, we will replicate the transformational process Courtney and I offer at these retreats. At the beginning of each chapter, I present the cultural context for how these beliefs and stories came to lodge in our minds. Then I pass the baton to Courtney, who will coach you through a process that will guide you to work with your own stories. We've found that teaming in this way creates a powerful and moving mechanism for making what's driving our lives apparent and visible—even *obvious.* Once you begin "to see what you're up to," to quote Courtney, you can work with the stories themselves and perform what she calls a "shift move," where you transform them into something that actually aligns with who you feel yourself to be and how you want to show up in the future. You can work this process as many times as you want in each section. To use an easy metaphor, we are onions. As you peel back layers of programming, you'll find even deeper layers beneath. We recommend going back again and again. Some of these chapters will feel like bigger bites than others—you might feel that the "Greed" chapter doesn't apply to you, for example, that you have an easy relationship with money. But we recommend doing the process in those sections anyway—we promise that you'll be surprised at what you'll uncover about yourself.

Each chapter is buttressed by additional tools that are specific to the sin or passion. We've learned these tools from all the visionary healers, thinkers, and therapists we've both been privileged to study with over the years. They are ideas that have been formative in our own lives and practices, and we are excited to share them with you.

THE CORE PROCESS

Courtney here. Each chapter of *On Our Best Behavior* examines particular stories associated with each of the Seven Deadly Sins—specifically, how each of these sins has become intertwined with our Western culture's definition of womanhood. In our years of learning, training, coaching, and teaching, we have come across various practices that are especially well suited to shifting one's relationship to each of these sins, and we offer those practices in each respective chapter of this workbook.

In *On Our Best Behavior,* Elise spoke to the larger issue of cultural inheritance and how each of us might go about the process of consciously choosing—rather than unconsciously receiving—the stories that shape our lives and create our identities. While each sin has had a particular influence upon our cultural notions of femininity, in this workbook we are offering a core set of tools that are essential to the larger process of claiming a conscious self. They will help each of you examine and redefine your relationship to specific aspects of your identity. As you move through this process, we hope you feel supported to discover and reorient your life to your own internal definition of what womanhood and wholeness mean.

Once excavated and named, every set of beliefs that we have inherited from our family, community, or broader culture creates an opportunity for us to consciously continue to internalize these belief systems or to shift and choose another set of foundational beliefs instead. One gift of *On Our Best Behavior* is that the book initiates this excavation and naming process. Many of our stories are the same, scripted even. As our stories about femininity become more conscious and explicit, we can shift them into something new. Once we see the stories we have been using to shape our behavior and guide our lives—most likely unwittingly—we have the opportunity to no longer be subject to them. We can begin to self-define our relationship to the balance between work and rest (sloth), ambition and desire (envy), self-love (pride), hunger and beauty (gluttony), money and material needs (greed), sexuality and pleasure (lust), anger, and sadness.

While each chapter of this workbook focuses on one of the deadly sins, we have developed a core process that will serve as the backbone of your inquiry and evolution. This process runs through every chapter and hinges on seven key tools, all of which I have been coaching, teaching, facilitating, and using in my own life for many years. As you practice these tools in each section of this book, we hope they become embodied. To that end, we've provided additional key takeaways so that you can extend their use to all parts of your life.

TOOL 1: IS IT A FACT OR IS IT A STORY?
Excavating Unconscious Stories

On Our Best Behavior describes many of the cultural ideals and norms we have internalized about womanhood and goodness. The first practice we offer in this workbook is to firmly identify these ideals and norms as what they are: stories, not facts.

When we can differentiate between fact and story, we restore our ability to distinguish between what is fixed and what is mutable. In everyday life, we regularly conflate fact and story. When we do this, we trick ourselves into believing that stories are as fixed, and *true,* as fact. When we treat stories as fact, their power grows. We become subject to the story, forgetting that one of our greatest powers as human beings lies in our ability to *choose* which stories we believe.

I first came across this deceptively simple yet powerful tool when I joined a forum hosted by the Conscious Leadership Group and began working with the book *The 15 Commitments of Conscious Leadership,* by Jim Dethmer, Diana Chapman, and Kaley Warner Klemp. It remains one of my go-to practices to help distinguish between what's real and what's not, to resolve conflict, and to remember my own agency. To distinguish between fact and story, I offer this simple definition:

- Facts are what a video recorder might capture about a situation.
- Stories are everything else.

That's it.

Stories are sometimes built upon facts and sometimes built upon thin air. It is also true that the same fact can often generate multiple, different stories (try this exercise with some friends: Throw out a fact and compare the stories you each generate from it). It is also true that, once we start to believe a story, we tend to focus on the facts that affirm the story rather than taking in facts that complicate it.

I'll give you an example: I came home the other day and my husband didn't look up from the table to say hi. This was a fact. The stories I immediately started telling myself were that he was angry with me, that I must have done something to piss him off, that we were definitely going to spend the rest of the night in a fight, and that maybe he didn't even want to be married anymore. (Extreme, but you can see how the mind starts to spin.) When I finally caught his attention, instead of attacking him for ignoring me, I said: "Hey, when you don't acknowledge me, I tell myself a story that you're upset with me." He looked at me for a second. "Ah, I'm sorry, Court—I had my AirPods in and was buried in my book—I didn't even hear you." This is a simple example, but helpful: When we let our stories run wild, we can lose touch with what's actually present.

When we're reading *On Our Best Behavior* or this workbook, it is helpful to remind ourselves that while many of the cultural beliefs we have internalized about the deadly sins may *feel* true, at the end of the day they remain stories. And the person who controls which stories I believe is me.

In each chapter of this workbook, we are going to encourage you to distinguish between facts and stories relevant to each of the deadly sins. You will learn to self-generate your own stories about each of the deadly sins, especially those that have particular resonance for you. Elise and I provide plenty of examples to help you get the hang of this critical concept.

Subsequent exercises in each chapter rely upon your having excavated the particular stories you currently believe about each of the deadly sins, so this first tool is foundational to many of the other practices that follow. We have provided lots of space for you to generate many stories about each of the deadly sins. However, as you make your way through subsequent exercises, we suggest you choose to focus on one to three stories per sin that you feel have the most potency, juice, or energetic charge in your life. You can always return and do the process with additional stories as they arise.

Key Takeaways from Tool 1

The concept of fact versus story is foundational to the core process used in this workbook. It's also a helpful tool to use in your everyday life. Here are some ways that we suggest you can make use of the distinction:

- Catch yourself when you're using a fact to make up a story. Pause and check in with others to see if the story matches their experience. Here's my example from the "Sloth" chapter: "Yes, it is true that I work thirty hours per week. It turns out that it's not true that I'm always behind." This practice works only if you're genuinely interested in learning if your story is correct.
- Use the language of fact versus story when speaking: "The fact is . . ." and "the story I make up about that fact is . . ." You may notice yourself becoming less rigid and more flexible with the stories you create. You might also find that you generate less conflict in your life and save time on unnecessary rumination.
- Broaden your storytelling: When you find yourself using a fact to generate a story, pause and ask yourself what other stories might be equally true. If you have friends, loved ones, or colleagues who consistently see the world differently than you do, ask yourself what their story might be

instead. For example, I have an optimistic friend whose voice I channeled when I had foot surgery. The fact is that 15 percent of people still experience pain one year after surgery. My story was that I needed to prepare for the worst. Her story was that, because I was going into the surgery with above-average health, my results were going to be above average as well. No need to worry. The point of this exercise is not to blindly believe the more optimistic story but to challenge yourself to hold both.

• Know your pattern. Over time, you may realize that you have a consistent tone to your stories. For example, some of us have a positivity bias, while some of us are more negative. Once you notice that you have a preference for a particular type of story, challenge yourself to see if there are any facts you are overlooking that could complicate your story.

TOOL 2: AND THEN WHAT?
Tracing the Acting, Sensing, Feeling, and Thinking Loop

Once we have identified our current stories about each of the deadly sins, we can track the effect that each of these stories has on our lives by looking at the habitual behaviors, body sensations, emotional states, and thinking patterns associated with each story.

While many of us treat our bodies, hearts, and minds as separate systems, in actuality they are all connected. Thoughts, in particular, have great power. They provoke certain behaviors, they arouse specific body sensations, they create and sustain emotional states, and they cause our minds to generate other ideas and beliefs.

Tool 2 enables us to become more explicit about the consequences of our current stories. Often, especially when a story or belief system operates in the background, we fail to notice just how much hold it has on us. For example, I moved to New York City just weeks after 9/11, and I started my professional career at a time when many of the city's industries, including mine, management consulting, were reeling from depressed earnings. This set of facts (plus my own inherent biases with which I made meaning of these facts) caused me to buy into the story that "my job security is fragile." The more I leaned into and believed this story, the more additional thoughts popped up, such as "You had better save up because you never know what might happen," "Be happy with any job you can get," and "Living in New York City is hard." The more I believed these stories, the more I interpreted other facts (such as any gaps between assignments) as additional proof of their validity. The more I believed these stories, the more time I spent at the office, the more money I saved, and the more I scrutinized every bill and purchase I made. The more I believed these stories, the more worried and less confident I felt at the office, and the more I related to my job from a place of stress rather than curiosity, growth, and opportunity. The more I related to my work from a place of stress, the more tense my body felt and the less I enjoyed my work. If you'd asked my twenty-five-year-old self what was going on, she likely would have replied that this state is just what living in New York City is like, without catching that it was a particular story that she had created and bought into that was really the driver behind the wheel.

Therefore, the point of Tool 2 is to bring awareness to all the ways a particular story shapes how we live our lives. In this part of the core process, we break down the lived experience created by the stories we buy into. We have broken down the power of stories to affect our behaviors, body sensations, emotions, and thought patterns into different steps and exercises on the pages that follow because many of us aren't used to checking in on these various aspects of our lived experience. As you practice and get the hang of Tool 2, though, you'll likely find that you're able to quickly work through and name the acting–sensing–feeling–thinking loop produced by any story. After you've tried working with Tool 2, we hope it becomes a regular practice for you that when you catch yourself in a story you ask yourself in quick succession: What actions does this story produce? What body sensations arise when I believe this story? What feelings arise when I believe this story? What additional thoughts does this story produce?

Step 1: What Actions Do You Take?

First, we ask you to consider and write down some of the actions you take and where you focus your time, attention, energy, and resources when you believe this current story. We also ask you to name a few real-time examples where this story has shown up and recently influenced your behavior.

To illustrate, here's an example from my own life: When I believe I don't have enough time, I speak impatiently to my children. When I believe I don't have enough time, I stay up late and wake up groggy. When I believe I don't have enough time, I start to prioritize my work over quality time with my friends and family. When I believe I don't have enough time, my attention goes to how busy I am and how much I am missing out on.

Step 2: What Sensations Do You Feel?

Second, we ask you to turn your attention inward and notice the specific body sensations aroused by a particular story. Paying attention to what our body is telling us through its arising sensations is a new and challenging practice for many of us. Books such as *The Body Keeps the Score* have introduced mainstream culture to the power of the information stored in the body. (Or we might say reintroduced; in truth, the body is our oldest intelligence system.) Katie and Gay Hendricks have been longtime pioneers in the field of somatic intelligence, and the tables we use throughout this book to help you find and name body sensations are adapted from exercises provided in their workshops.

When I choose to believe this story, I experience the following sensations in my body:

In my forehead, I feel:

Swirling	Fogginess	Buzziness
Spaciousness	Density	Sharpness
Scattered	Throbbing	Stirred up

In the back of my neck, across my shoulders, and in my jaw, I feel:

Tight	Twisted	Pulling
Bunched	Itchy	Burning
Cord-like	Clenched	Steely
Rigid	Blocky	Prickly

Across my high chest and upper throat, I feel:

Heaviness	Constriction	Cut off
Closed in	Numb	Melting
Compressed	Achy	Pierced
Unable to breathe	Flatness	Cold

Around the stomach area, I feel:

Knotted	Fluttering	Butterflies
Nauseous	Braced	Hollow
Churning	Empty	Doubled-over

In other parts of my body, I feel:

Racing heart	Trembling hands	Low-energy
Collapsed	Wiggly	Teary
Expanded	Tingly	Stretched

These tables are adapted from Gay and Katie Hendricks's work on body sensations and intelligence. See www.hendricks.com for further information.

For many of us, this is a challenging practice. We are used to relating to our body as an activity machine, and we have developed numerous strategies to ignore, numb, or dissociate from its sensations. Many of us have stories about body sensations: They are uncomfortable or painful, and we fear that, if we acknowledge these sensations, they may prove inconvenient or slow us down.

One way we collude with the stories we have inherited from our families, communities, and culture and ensure that these stories remain firmly in place is by failing to acknowledge and be with the physical sensations they produce. In contrast, when we tune into the body sensations produced by our stories, we begin to experience each story's full weight and cost. As we bring forward and name the stories that we have been unconsciously choosing to animate our lives, the question becomes what stories we will consciously choose instead. When we reacquaint ourselves with the sensations of our bodies, we are encountering important information that we can use to determine which stories serve us, which stories internally resonate with us, and which stories are authentic to who we are rather than inheritances from the external world.

In my own life, I grew up as someone who was known for her mind, and for many years my self-concept would have looked something like a lollipop. My body was here only as a stick to carry my head around. In my own process of unfolding and growth, the rediscovery of my body's intelligence has been one of my biggest ahas. My daily meditation practice is now centered on attending to the sensations of my body. This is a practice I find grounding, but one other consequence of it is that body sensations now regularly inform my decision-making throughout the day.

As one small example, I agreed to work on a professional project with a friend of mine nearly a year ago. As the timeline emerged for the project, it became clear that I did not have as much time available for the project as my friend hoped for. Disappointing others is something that feels uncomfortable for me. I can feel a hard knot in my stomach and a clenching in my throat develop even as I write these words and hearken back to this memory. These body sensations are so uncomfortable for me that I elected to keep working on the project rather than speak to my friend about my overcommitments. At the same time, the more I worked on the project and the more I disregarded the limits of my own energy, the more tired and overextended I felt. I also started to experience growing waves of nausea every time I prioritized not feeling the pain of disappointing my friend over the pain of disrespecting my own body and mind's limitations. The nausea ultimately became so significant and loud that I realized I needed to speak with my friend and reveal my truth. Having that hard conversation with her was the peak of my physical discomfort, but the nausea, tight throat, and knotty stomach have not come back since.

Step 3: What Feelings Do You Have?

The third step in Tool 2 is continuing to go inward, this time paying attention to the emotions that arise when you believe and invest in a story. Much like the physical sensations we tend to overlook and numb ourselves to, many of us have a well-developed habit of skipping over our emotions, finding them inconvenient, embarrassing, or shameful. This is problematic, because ignoring our emotional responses is another way we unconsciously keep inherited stories firmly entrenched within us, rather than excavating them and examining their full cost.

The practice here is to name and be with the emotions that arise when we find ourselves in the grip of a particular story. Our culture tends to devalue emotions as valuable feedback, but they are really an essential part of the human experience, and we have a rich and varied vocabulary to describe them. However, my experience has been that, when we use a sophisticated word to describe what we're feeling rather than just naming it plain, that fancy vocabulary serves to distance us from the feeling rather than bringing us closer to our own lived emotional experience.

Therefore, in this section of each chapter, we invite you to name the emotion that arises when you believe a specific story. We also invite you to view your feeling as a variant of one of four core emotions: anger, fear, sadness, and joy. We have borrowed the feeling scale that the Conscious Leadership Group uses as the tool to help you find which of these four core emotions you're experiencing with respect to each story and deadly sin.

When I choose to believe this story, I experience the following emotions:

Anger

LOW	MEDIUM	HIGH
Annoyed	Agitated	Enraged
Bored	Disgusted	Furious
Bothered	Frustrated	Hostile
Dissatisfied	Indignant	Livid
Irritable	Irritated	Outraged
Tense	Resentful	Vengeful

Sadness

LOW	MEDIUM	HIGH
Blue	Discouraged	Agony
Down	Gloomy	Anguished
Lonely	Hopeless	Devastated
Somber	Melancholic	Heartbroken
Solemn	Regretful	Grief-stricken
Unhappy	Sorrowful	Mourning

Fear

LOW	MEDIUM	HIGH
Concerned	Apprehensive	Frightened
Guarded	Edgy	Frozen
Hesitant	Jumpy	Panicked
Reluctant	Nervous	Petrified
Suspicious	Startled	Shocked
Vulnerable	Worried	Terrified

Joy

LOW	MEDIUM	HIGH
Calm	Cheerful	Blissful
Carefree	Excited	Delighted
Content	Graceful	Ecstatic
Lighthearted	Optimistic	Enthusiastic
Peaceful	Proud	Elated
Relaxed	Thankful	Expansive

These tables are excerpted with permission from the Conscious Leadership Group's work on emotions. See www.conscious.is for further information.

We want to acknowledge that academics have devoted volumes to parsing out and categorizing the range of human emotional experience, and we have diverged slightly from the Conscious Leadership Group in our own presentation of the four core emotions. For the purposes of this workbook, we are going to stick with anger, fear, sadness, and joy. These four emotions are associated with predictable and consistent physiological patterns of sensations. Other emotions, such as jealousy, are combinations of these four core emotions and have variable and context-specific associated physiological sensations.

Most important, we have chosen to focus on anger, fear, sadness, and joy because our primary goal with this practice is to bring you closer to your own emotional experience. We have found that the simpler the language, the more connected you are to your own heart.

Step 4: What Thoughts Come Next?

The last step in Tool 2 is to track the additional thoughts and stories that arise when you believe a particular thought. Stories are world-generating; that is part of their power. One single story can serve as the foundation for a whole set of assumptions we have about ourselves, another person, or a situation. The invitation here is to become curious and specific about the chain of thoughts that each story produces. Often, when we believe a particular thought, it causes us to move backward in time. We return to a memory of something that happened in the past, and we relive and retell the experience. Other times, when we believe a particular thought, it causes us to move forward in time and to predict and catastrophize about what might happen. When we double down on stories, judgments also typically arise about ourselves and others, and these judgments have a life of their own.

For example, when I choose to believe the story that I need to be thin to be attractive, my mind goes back in time to memories of myself when I was in junior high school, heavier than I am today, and how uncomfortable and unattractive I felt. When I believe the story equating thinness with attractiveness, my mind moves forward in time and I anticipate how difficult it is going to be to maintain my weight as I age. I also start to judge and think less of myself if I overeat when

I am caught in the throes of this story. I become more vigilant about my food choices, and eating becomes less fun.

My exploration of my own stories has been greatly influenced by Byron Katie's process called The Work, a simple yet extremely powerful methodology grounded in her realization that stories are the root of our suffering rather than reality itself. The tools she offers in The Work are available for free on her website and inspire the questions we pose in this section of each chapter.

Key Takeaways from Tool 2

Tool 2 breaks down the four ways that stories wield their power: through the actions, body sensations, feelings, and thoughts they produce. That said, the point of these practices is not to segment and separate actions, body sensations, feelings, and thoughts from one another. Instead, our goal is for you to go into the full, lived experience of when, where, and how a story shows up and drives your life. This is the second step in the core process of this workbook because, once we've excavated and named a story, we want to treat these stories with respect. They have likely been with us for a long while, and we've been unaware of their full influence.

This workbook is about what it means to shift from being a "good" human to being a "whole" one. One way we reclaim our wholeness as a human being is to fully and unconditionally witness and accept our internal experience. Our experience as human beings includes what we're sensing in our bodies, feeling in our hearts, and thinking in our minds. The process of slowing down to take stock of each aspect of ourselves, to value each one, to welcome and not push any of them away—even sensations we've been conditioned to code as "bad"—is essential for coming into a relationship with yourself as a whole person.

In addition to going through the steps of Tool 2 in each chapter of this workbook, we suggest that you regularly name the sensations of your body and the feelings of your heart as difficult moments arise in your everyday life. Too often, we live in the land of the mind—thoughts, belief, and story. We invite you to rebalance your experience of what it means to be human by including the body and emotions.

TOOL 3: WHY STORIES STICK

Identifying the Underlying Fear

Once we have identified the actions, body sensations, emotions, and thoughts that arise when we believe a particular story, often our first reaction is to say, "How can I get rid of this thing?" You may find that this is easier said than done. We've been carrying around stories about womanhood and goodness for a long time, and with good reason. When you find a story sticking around way past its expiration date, the likely reason is that it's riding on the back of fear. As we just explored in the previous section, when we choose to believe many of the stories we have about the seven (or eight) sins, we feel anger, sadness, fear, or joy. However, the alternative—to identify an inherited story and then to exchange it for a different story more internally derived—causes us to feel emotions too. One of those emotions, more often than not, is fear.

As human beings, we're evolutionarily disposed to see the world through the lens of threat. It's what has kept us alive as a species. As you may have discovered when you explored the body sensations associated with some of your stories, the physiological experience of fear is *uncomfortable*. Why? Because fear is designed to capture our attention and motivate us to devote all our energy and resources to do whatever it takes to feel safe again.

The experience of feeling threat in the body is so significant that we can use a shorthand developed by the Conscious Leadership Group to describe its presence. They call it going "below the line." Tip-offs that we're experiencing a situation from below the line include:

- Bracing, contraction, or any rigidity in the body
- Holding our breath
- Feeling defensive, closed, or guarded
- Worrying
- Rigid thinking: using a lens of either/or
- Life-or-death thinking: using a lens of "This is super serious"

It's important to notice when we're below the line or when we're experiencing a situation from a place of threat because the sensations of fear are so strong that they hijack our body and dictate the way we show up in the world.

That fear is why stories of womanhood and goodness stick around and can be so difficult to dislodge. If we want to discard an inherited cultural norm about how a good woman acts, we have to be willing to face and be with the fears that arise from choosing to go our own way.

For example, I took several years off from professional, paid work when my husband and I started having children. In retrospect, I made this choice because I had internalized the ideal that "good moms put their children first" and I couldn't figure out how to meet this ideal and work at the same time. But if you'd asked me at the time to name out loud why I chose to stay home, I wouldn't have been able to voice this story at all. In fact, I would have told you that I supported women who become parents and continue to work at the same time. Despite my mind purporting to believe that women could do both, this story had nonetheless unconsciously lodged itself in my body and was dictating my choices. As I spent my time with our children and running our household, I became increasingly unhappy and resentful, but it took me several years to realize that I had to face and be with my fears around motherhood if I wanted to reenter the workforce. I couldn't live in alignment with the story my conscious mind believed and what my body and heart were telling me they wanted until I met and wrestled with the fear that kept an old, unconscious story stuck in the driver's seat. (I've shared this example from my own life to illustrate how fear drives our attachment to old stories, even as these stories ultimately don't serve us. However, I want to acknowledge that I had the opportunity to choose whether to work or stay at home in the first place, and many women do not.)

The ability to name, face, and be with the fears that undergird our allegiance to rigid and outdated notions of womanhood is one of the most powerful takeaways we hope all women get from using this workbook. In each chapter, Elise and I will continue to provide examples for each of the sins where we've had to name, face, and be with our fears so that you can see how potent a tool this is. We're doing our work right alongside you.

Many of us have a narrow definition of fear and believe it arises only under extreme circumstances, such as when an airplane dips and dives. However, the cues of fears are actually more subtle, nuanced, and broad than we typically understand. As we stated earlier, the objective of fear is to get us to act in a way that keeps us safe. While the academic study of fear is in its infancy, many researchers believe that human beings have evolved five sets of behaviors that we use as strategies for safety: Fight, Flee, Freeze, Faint, and Fawn. Each of these five strategies has its own physiological signature designed to produce different sets of behaviors.

The Fight response is designed to get us to attack and go on the offense in the presence of threat. In action, the Fight response looks big, angry, and intense. **The Flee response** is designed to get us to sprint to safety in the presence of threat. In action, the Flee response looks like behaviors of withdrawal, avoidance, quick action, and separation. Because many predators use movement to detect their prey, **the Freeze response** is designed to get us to not move in the presence of threat. In action, the Freeze response is the startle reflex, holding your breath and failing to act or move. **The Fawn response,** found only in highly social creatures, is designed to get us to seek protection from others in the presence of threat. In action, the Fawn response is about appeasing and accommodating someone else, even if that someone else may also be the one scaring you. Last, because many predators discard prey that is already dead, **the Faint response** is designed to get us to act like a rag doll in the presence of threat. In action, the Faint response looks like collapse, despair, and lack of agency.

Many of us exhibit a combination of these five flavors of fear; others may experience several of them chronologically. You may also find that you reliably exhibit one kind of fear in some contexts and another kind of fear in others.

You don't need to master the definitions of these five flavors of fear or understand exactly when one arises, in what order, or in what combination. Instead, the point of describing them is to broaden our understanding of what fear looks and feels like in the body so that we can more accurately identify when it's present. I was introduced to four of the fear flavors (Fight, Flee, Freeze, and Faint) in workshops taught by Katie Hendricks, and the corresponding columns in the table on page 25 are excerpted from her Evolutionary Playground training manual. From my own experience with clients in workshops and group and private work, I have elected to expand the flavors of fear to include the Fawn response as well.

The Five Flavors of Fear

FIGHT	FLEE	FREEZE	FAWN	FAINT
Defensive	Leaving the scene	Freezing up	Fixing	Fatigue
Short-fused	Checking out	Feeling stuck	Appeasing	Fuzziness
Guarded	Withdrawing	Unable to think	Accommodating	Fogginess
Rigid attitude	Hiding	Unable to speak	Deference	Blanking out
Pushing back	Distracting	Deer in the headlights	Solicitous	Overwhelmed
Triggered	Avoiding	Tensing up	Looking to others	Weighed down
Edgy	Pulling away	Flinching	People-pleasing	Collapsed
Agitated	Analyzing	Panicked	Trouble saying no	Drained
Frustrated	Diagnosing	Hesitating	Pacifying	Feeling helpless
Skeptical	Distancing	Startle reflex	Making excuses	Despairing
Criticizing	Nervous	Paralyzed	Minimizing your size/role	Hopeless
Blaming	Worried	Terrified	Wingman role	Powerless
Judging	Frantic	Confusion	Downplaying	Cold feet
Arguing	Anxious	Unable to decide	Smiling on the outside	Numb
Intensity	Dreading	Holding your breath	Flattery	Exhausted
Loud voice	Acting quickly	Unsure what to do	Walking on eggshells	Burned out
Puffed up body	Going into the head	In shock	Ignoring your needs	Passive

Excerpted from Gay and Katie's Evolutionary Playground workshop materials, with the exception of the "Fawn" column. See www.hendricks.com for further information.

Just as we have broadened our understanding of how fear manifests in the body and through action, we want to expand our understanding of what scares us in the first place. There are three fundamental human fears that can become activated in all of us. When any of these are put at risk, we experience a situation from a place of threat:

- Fear of loss of security
- Fear of loss of approval
- Fear of loss of control

Loss of security means we're afraid that something physically or emotionally painful might happen to us or to our loved ones. **Loss of approval** means we're afraid that others will judge us unfavorably. Human beings know they must remain part of a tribe to survive. We have biologically evolved to scan and read for cues that the tribe may reject us, making us especially attuned to social judgment and biologically wired for approval. **Loss of control** means we're afraid someone or something is getting in the way of our agenda or plan for how things "need to go." Human beings use our capacity for agency, activity, and achievement as a tactic to make sure we stay safe, and when our control plan is put at risk, we become scared.

As you excavate stories about the deadly sins in each of their respective chapters, we're going to ask you to explore the relationship of each of these stories to fear. We'll ask you to name the fear response that feels associated with each story, and we'll ask you to imagine what seems at risk and what you're worried might happen if you were to leave each of these stories behind. Finally, we'll ask you to consider whether this fear is related to a threat to your need for security, approval, or control.

Key Takeaways from Tool 3

The goal of this exercise is not to make fear go away. On the contrary, it is to bring fear out into the daylight. As you may discover, inherited stories about womanhood and the deadly sins get their power from the fears lying underneath them. And you may also be surprised to discover that the biggest antidote to fear is the simple act of facing and being with it.

While we are examining stories about womanhood in this workbook, one takeaway from Tool 3 is just how often fear dictates our choices in all aspects of our life. Therefore, you can use your expanded understanding of how fear manifests and what triggers a threat response to see just how often fear is present and when you've gone below the line in everyday life.

Even subtle degrees of threat are designed to cause us to prioritize feeling safe over experiencing other states, such as love, connection, curiosity, creativity, and aliveness. The more skilled we become at identifying fear and the more accepting we become of just how often it shows up in our lives, the more adept we become at not letting it dictate our actions and behaviors. Ironically, the stronger our relationship with fear, the less powerful it becomes. As our connection to our experience of fear grows stronger, we are more able to make conscious choices and live our lives in alignment with the values and priorities that we care about most.

TOOL 4: WELCOME TO THE DRAMA TRIANGLE
Relating to Stories from Victimhood Consciousness

When we're experiencing life from below the line or from a state of threat and not conscious as to what's happening, fear ends up driving our choices. When fear dictates our behavior, we default to focusing on safety. When this happens, situations start repeating themselves because we're looking at things through a lens of fear and safety rather than considering what issues need to be learned and what issues need to be resolved. To that end, one big tip-off that we're experiencing a situation from a place of threat is when we find ourselves in a repeating dynamic. The pattern itself suggests we're letting fear dictate our behavior—we're solving for safety rather than for a deeper issue.

Stephen Karpman, a psychologist working in the 1960s, dubbed these repeating patterns the Drama Triangle. When we see the world through a lens of fear and we're stuck in these recurring patterns, there are three roles that we assign ourselves and others: Victim, Villain, and Hero. These roles are about reacting to the feeling of threat and solving for safety in our lives.

Another shorthand for saying that I'm experiencing life from a place of threat is to say that "I'm at the effect of the world," meaning I believe that external conditions determine how I'm feeling and doing, and I can't feel safe unless I manage, respond, or react to what's happening outside of me. The Drama Triangle describes the three roles we adopt and the corresponding beliefs and actions we take on when we let fear that arises in response to a situation dictate our experience.

While only one of these roles has the official name of **Victim,** in truth, all three roles are flavors of victimhood because all three roles are about reacting from a place of threat. Each role describes a particular strategy for dealing with fear and feeling at the effect of the world. All three roles are ultimately about believing that external circumstances dictate your internal sense of well-being. The three roles may have different beliefs about their own agency and thus very different patterns of behavior, but all three roles share a belief that something has to change in the outside world in order for them to be okay.

The first role in the Drama Triangle is the **Victim.** There are real victims in the world; terrible things have happened to these individuals. But what we're talking about here is a broader mindset of being at the effect of the world and relating to it as a Victim, through the lens of victim consciousness. The Victim feels a powerlessness, a lack of agency, and an inability to assert and change reality. Victims tend to complain and argue for why they're never going to get what they want.

The second role within the Drama Triangle is the **Villain.** When the Villain feels signals of threat arising in their body, they develop a very strong belief about who is to blame, what needs to change, and what needs to happen for this feeling of threat to go away. The Villain can blame themselves or they can blame others, but the key here is that the Villain's strategy is to mitigate fear and feel safe again by feeling certain, definitive, and right.

The third role is the **Hero.** The Hero responds to the signals of threat arising in their body by trying to relieve these feelings of fear for themselves and for others. The key, however, is that these strategies bring only temporary relief. The situation repeats itself, and fear returns. The Hero has two primary methods through which they mitigate the sensations of fear. The first is to use techniques of distraction and avoidance with themselves and with others to dampen the discomfort of fear. These distraction strategies can be obvious, such as drugs or alcohol, but Heroes might also distract themselves with excuse-making or with minimizing statements such as "This isn't that big of a deal" or "I can handle this." The second method for Heroes is that they take on responsibilities that are not theirs while ignoring actions that address the root cause of a recurring pattern. Heroing efforts often *appear* helpful, but the fact that the situation keeps repeating is a tip-off that their efforts are merely temporary fixes rather than actual solutions.

When we're experiencing a situation through the lens of the Drama Triangle, we can adopt the language and tone of one role at a time, we can play multiple roles simultaneously, or we can bounce back and forth between roles. Moreover, when we take on a particular role, we also end up assigning others to the other roles. Heroes need people to help and comfort, so they view others as Victims. Victims feel powerless, so they need others to take on the role of Villain and Hero on their behalf.

Typical Phrases Used by the Three Roles of the Drama Triangle

VICTIM	VILLAIN	HERO
"I'm trying" "I'm so tired and overwhelmed"	"It's obvious what we should do" "Here's how we got into this mess"	"You can count on me" "I'll help you figure this out"
"I'm so confused"	"Here's the source of this problem"	"Look on the bright side"
"I don't know what else to do"	"I screwed up"	"I can handle this"
"I have to . . . "	"What's wrong with me/ them?"	"It's easier if I just take care of this"
"I don't have a choice"	"You just don't get it"	"I don't want to upset anyone"
"This is so hard"	"We have to do it this way"	"You can't do this without me"
"This is the way it is"	"I'm right and you're wrong"	"This is no big deal"

This table is adapted with permission from the Conscious Leadership Group's work on the Drama Triangle. See www.conscious.is for further information.

As we work through the stories associated with each of the deadly sins in subsequent chapters, you might notice yourself defaulting to relating to these stories through the lens of the Drama Triangle. There are many payoffs to seeing life from this perspective. Many of us have become accustomed to the short-term energy spike that acting from a state of threat can elicit. We get to blame others for where we are in our lives rather than taking responsibility. We get to experience the pleasure of certainty and righteousness. We stick with patterns and roles that, while uncomfortable, feel familiar. We often maintain connection with others through collective commiseration in the style of the three Drama Triangle roles. Above all, we get to avoid truly experiencing the full cost of living from fear.

Moreover, when our culture talks about the evolving norms of womanhood or, frankly, almost any political or social issue, the Drama Triangle tends to be our default perspective and language. As a sidenote, now that you've learned the Drama Triangle, it can be a fun exercise to watch any news show, no matter the channel and no matter the political orientation, and see the Drama Triangle play out in real time.

When we explore culturally inherited ideals for womanhood and where they come from, it is tempting to blame the media, men, our ancestors, our politicians, and so on. It is true that many of these people have played a role in our cultural notions of femininity, and we hope they take stock of their beliefs and actions and make conscious decisions going forward. But what we *really* want is for readers of this workbook to feel that they have the power and resources to make changes in their own lives that enable them to lead the lives they truly and desperately want—without needing anyone or anything else to change first.

When I first learned the Drama Triangle at the Conscious Leadership Group, I was wrestling with a disagreement that my husband and I were having. I was approaching the situation from a place of threat, and I was below the line. I was invited to stand up and talk about the issue while physically embodying each of its three roles. My coach Grace placed signposts for the roles of Victim, Villain, and Hero on the ground, and I physically toggled back and forth between them, literally walking the Drama Triangle. I felt a huge release of energy as I played the roles of Victim, Villain, and Hero head on (it was actually kind of liberating and fun), but I also could sense in my body just how trapped I was by my stories and by my fear.

While the process outlined in the chapters is not dynamic—you don't have to play it out in this way—we wanted to give you an example of what this looks like in real time. Just a note that we're conscious that we're giving you family examples—and some readers won't relate—but in the interest of picking on people in our lives who can take it, bear with us. This is from an episode I did with Elise on *Pulling the Thread* where I coached her through the Drama Triangle live: Once you've practiced with this book, you'll become adept at recognizing the roles you're playing in real time as well.

COURTNEY: [*Note: I was feeling pretty angry and looking for someone to blame when we began this exercise, so I started with playing the Villain.*] First of all, if you want to know who I'm mad at, I'm mad at the schools. I'm mad that we give a quarter of the year off to students. And by the way, have you seen the statistics? Students forget a third of what they learned the previous year because summer is super long. Is it the teachers' unions? Is it tradition? Why do we keep living in this stupid system when we have the evidence that we shouldn't be giving kids thirteen weeks off, yet we still do it over and over and over again?

Now I'm going to shift into Victim mode, which is: Well, this is just the way it is. This is the structure of our country. School's been run this way for a hundred years. There's absolutely nothing I can do about this.

Because of this, I have to figure out thirteen weeks of summer plans for my three children. If I don't do that, they're going to sit around while I'm trying to work all day. They're going to be bugging me, and I'm not going to get my work done, and then I'm going be forced to make them get on a device, and then they're going to become addicted to their devices. Then I'm going to have to deal with the fact that now they're addicted to Fortnite or Roblox, and not only is this affecting me and my ability to do my job, but this is affecting the health and well-being of my children. So now, not only am *I* a victim, but my children are the victims of this stupid national system we have as well because *there's nothing that they can do.* They have no choice but to lie around the house all day on their devices.

Then I'm going to shift into Hero mode, which looks like: I'm going to scurry around and work really hard to overschedule them. I'm going to put them at camp every single week. I may or may not ask my husband to do this with me, as this has been the role I've played for a long time.

I could then move into another Drama Triangle about the gendered roles of who's doing what in our household, because I'm going to be the one who's up until midnight researching camps, and figuring out what camp would be the perfect one, and desperately trying to secure a spot, because I can't bear the thought of our children hanging out and doing nothing all summer, because that would be terrible for them and terrible for me.

ELISE: Oh, Courtney, this is so relatable. Here's what I'm below the line about. I'm going to pick on my husband Rob because everyone knows I love Rob. So, our school has two spring breaks, which is kind of nice—one of them is in February, so we decided to go home to Montana to ski. I'm going to start with Villain mode, but you can tell me what I'm really up to.

Okay, so the kids have this week off, and clearly I'm the only one who's going to take the initiative to plan something. If I don't plan something, then nothing will happen. The time will arrive too quickly. We'll have no place to stay. We'll have no flight. I can't rely on Rob to research anything or book anything. He would interrupt me here to remind me that he *did* book the rental car and actually fought with the rental car company because they tried to downgrade us, which was unacceptable because we had very much overpaid. When I saw how much he paid for the rental, Courtney, I flipped out a little bit because *who does that?* But at the same time, he did take the initiative—after I asked several times—to book it. So, who am I to criticize? Other than that, I organized everything. I did all the meal planning. I booked all of our flights. I booked our Airbnb. I organized our parking at the airport. I organized the ski rentals, the ski school, the cat sitter, the lift tickets . . .

COURTNEY: Hero. Hero. Hero.

ELISE: I made sure that my kids had extra ski socks. I packed them completely. And then, you know, Rob, of course, was like, "Where are we going? What's the plan?" Then I had to get really mad because it's in the calendar that we share. Why do I have to go back through my email when I've already sent him all of this? Why am I the only one who prereads the directions for how to get into the condo? It will never change.

COURTNEY: Victim.

ELISE: If I drop these balls, then nothing will ever happen and we'll never go anywhere, and my kids will also just be on Fortnite and Roblox all day. And not only that, but they will spend more money than we would going on a trip on Roblox and V-Bucks, because all they do is treat me like an ATM.

We promise, the Drama Triangle is really fun. It's Tool 4 in the core process. We'll take you through a similar process with the stories you identify in each of the following chapters. Whether you stand up and use the prompts we've given you to discover for yourself what the roles of Victim, Villain, and Hero actually feel like to you, or whether you prefer to continue journaling in this workbook, the point of this exercise is to create a space where the language of victimhood can be fully expressed. Discover for yourself whether this is a space you'd like to just visit or one you'd like to remain in with respect to your story. It's ultimately your choice.

Key Takeaways from Tool 4

Once you learn the Drama Triangle, it's kind of hard to unsee it. When you catch yourself using the language of the Victim, Villain, or Hero in your everyday life, it's a sign you're approaching the issue from a place of threat and a signal for you to tune in to what you're really afraid of.

If you catch yourself in any recurring pattern, whether it's a disagreement with a business colleague or an issue with a child or partner leaving wet towels on the floor, any repeating situation is a ripe opportunity to pull out the Drama Triangle and use the questions of Tool 4 to understand the role you're playing in the dynamic.

If you find yourself locked into the role of Victim, Villain, or Hero and are unwilling to see the world any other way, then you might ask yourself what payoffs you get from using this lens to view the world. Bonus points if you're willing to call yourself out as committed to approaching a situation from the lens of victimhood, since that's what the Drama Triangle is all about.

TOOL 5: WHAT DO THESE STORIES GET YOU?
Owning the Payoffs and Costs of Our Unconscious Stories

When we uncover a story that we've internalized from our family, community, and culture that has been driving our choices, it can be tempting to stay in the blame and shame (blame directed internally) game. Both blame and shame, however, function to keep us from doing anything differently and keep us locked in choices driven by fear.

We might say that both blame and shame share a similar assumption: that the stories we uncovered are a problem and that there is something wrong with us for having let these stories dictate our lives. However, if the ultimate goal of this workbook is to not have to perform to some rigid externally derived norm of femininity in order to feel "good" and instead to regain a state of wholeness, or unconditional acceptance of all aspects of oneself, then shaming the parts of us that internalized and bought into cultural ideals of womanhood doesn't get us very far.

It is true that, now that we have unearthed and explored the stories we've inherited, we may make different choices and cultivate new stories. It is true that we may be ready to face our fears and choose other priorities and values to live from. It is true that our previous choices may have cost us in various ways. It is *also* true that our previous choices were likely adaptive and intelligent in their origin. It is *also* true that our previous choices came with certain benefits and payoffs and served some purpose for a time. It is *also* true that letting inherited stories dictate our choices, at some level, got us to the point where we're now in the position to ask anew whether we'd like to choose differently going forward.

Tool 5 is a series of questions we present that are designed to help you appreciate your past choices while simultaneously sitting with their consequences and helping you look forward to what comes next. Inspired by my work with the Conscious Leadership Group, these questions are:

- Who taught me this story?
- What do I gain from believing this story?
- In what way does believing this story serve me?
- Who do I get to stay close to by believing this story?
- How do I keep this story going?
- If I didn't believe this story, what would I be doing instead?
- What does this story cost me?
- If I discard this story, what do I have to risk?
- How do I use this story to keep me from devoting my energy to that which makes me feel truly alive?

- In order to discard this story, what role, behavior, or way of being do I need to shed and grow out of?
- How would my relationship to myself change if I didn't believe this story?
- How would my relationship to [insert name] change if I didn't believe this story?

These questions are adapted with permission from the Conscious Leadership Group's work on the Drama Triangle. See www.conscious.is for further information.

As you work through these questions for each story, we hope you find compassion for yourself for why you've chosen to believe this story for so long. At the same time, we hope you can appreciate how you may benefit from letting this story go. For example, when I reflected many years ago on my decision to stay at home with my children when they were little, I realized that, by defaulting back to an outdated cultural norm that "good mothers put their children first" to determine my actions, I got to avoid and postpone a difficult reckoning with myself. I came to face that I didn't know what I wanted to do professionally and that I felt unsatisfied and insecure about my ability to contribute and distinguish myself in the field of consulting. Staying at home with my children, while it made me unhappy and resentful, also enabled me to avoid looking at some uncomfortable truths about myself.

Rather than seeing the choices each of us made in the past through a lens of shame, we invite you to view these choices through a lens of respect and curiosity. In respecting the choices of our past, we accept all parts of ourselves and cultivate a return to the unconditional acceptance of self that is our birthright.

We hope this workbook enables you to thoughtfully create and choose the stories with which you align your actions going forward. We do not offer the tools of this workbook from the vantage point that there was something wrong with the version of you that was here before; rather, we're curious about what gets created when women refuse to reject *any* aspect of themselves as "wrong" or "in need of fixing." The goal is to generate—from a place of *wholeness*—our own stories to live by.

Key Takeaway from Tool 5

The questions in Tool 5 are designed to get you to look at a particular situation or issue with fresh eyes. They are great prompts you can use anytime to identify a story you'd like to explore or anytime you find yourself in a challenging circumstance. The questions can be used to supplement any inquiry into fear (Tool 3) or exploration of the Drama Triangle (Tool 4) as well.

TOOL 6: TEACH THE CLASS
Reclaiming Responsibility and Becoming the Creator

When we experience a situation from a place of threat, we let external circumstances and the fears that arise in response to those circumstances determine our experience. In other words, we're at the effect of these circumstances. We can also say that when we're Below the Line, inhabiting the roles of the Drama Triangle, and viewing the world from the lens of victimhood consciousness, we're experiencing life as happening *to us*. As we explored in Tools 4 and 5, there are plenty of payoffs from approaching life this way, but there are many costs as well. When the scales finally tip and the costs of living from fear become greater than our gains, the question becomes, How do we swap out the lens of victimhood? And how do we find a new way to see and experience the world? That new way can be thought of as living above the line.

Life from above the line looks pretty different. Here we live from a state of trust. Rather than feeling closed, defensive, guarded, rigid, serious, and anxious, from above the line we feel open, curious, flexible, responsive, playful, and secure. We're able to access higher values such as creativity, connection, love, purpose, and integrity to guide our life choices. From above the line we still feel fear, but we're aware of when it arises. We don't push away its sensations. Instead, we welcome all emotions as part of the human experience, but we choose to not let those emotions drive our reactivity.

Most important, we shift from experiencing life as happening *to us* to experiencing life as happening *for us* and *by us*. Rather than feeling stuck in the various roles and lenses of victimhood, when we choose to shift and experience life from above the line, we take responsibility for our lived experience. We reclaim our agency, power, and status as the ultimate creator of our life. We understand, *I am the one who chooses which stories inform my life, I am the one who chooses whether fear or something greater dictates my actions,* and *Even as there are things about life that I cannot control, I am the one who chooses how to make meaning out of those facts.*

When we're stuck in the Drama Triangle or we're attached to a story because it's been with us for such a long time, it can feel hard to see the world differently and to claim our personal responsibility. Therefore, in Tool 6, we serve up a playful approach out of this morass.

Called "Teach the Class," this exercise is the ultimate jiu-jitsu maneuver. It's one of my favorite tools that I learned from the Conscious Leadership Group because it asks you to claim responsibility for all the ways you've set up your life to ensure that you experience it from a place of threat. The list you create becomes your new playbook with at least a half-dozen action steps, any one of which you could take to shift your experience of life from Victim to Creator.

To set up this practice, once you've identified a particular story for each of the sins, you will pretend that you have been invited to a women-only college to teach a class on how to subscribe to the exact same story that you are working with. Your students need very specific instructions that they can follow to re-create and live by this story in their own lives. This practice of teaching imaginary students is designed to help you take responsibility and see yourself as the ultimate creator of your life but with a little dose of humor along the way. So have fun with this tool!

Here's a spotlight on "Teach the Class" in practice.

ELISE: Good morning, class! Thank you for enrolling in this once-in-a-lifetime learning opportunity. I'm thrilled to teach you all how to engineer your life so you can live and die by this edict: "I'm the only one who can do it right, therefore I should do it all." This is a rule to live by! It's such a great rule that it means I'm your professor in every class this year—and your custodian, dining room attendant, and dean—because nobody else can do it as well as me!

So first, you want to make sure that you choose a partner who is noncompetitive by nature—you wouldn't want this person to think that there's *anything* they could do better. Then, before they even get to try doing something— responding to a school email, booking a vacation, scheduling their own annual physical—rush to do it first. You wouldn't want them to get a hint of their own competence! This is critical: *do everything fast* to assert your supremacy. You need to train them in learned helplessness. Pretty soon, because they've never done anything and don't know the process, protocols, or contacts, you'll be responsible for . . . everything! Sweet!

This is even easier at work: Yes, you might have to "collaborate" cross-functionally. But if it's in your domain, hold everything close to your chest. Refuse to delegate. Don't share any of your work—because why would you accept support when you need to do it all yourself in order for it to be done right? What would happen if someone did it . . . better? You can't have that! Don't allow it! Lock your office door!

Key Takeaway from Tool 6

We chose a women's college as the place for you to "Teach the Class" for a specific reason: While we tend to think of culture as this vague, amorphous "thing," in reality we pass it from person to person. Most of us picked up the patterns and stories we live by from other women, whether it's our mothers, grandmothers, friends, or even public figures. In turn, we are modeling our stories for our own daughters and sons. While we'll encourage you throughout this workbook *not* to triangulate exercises through other people—to claim your wanting for yourself, for example, and not on behalf of someone else—"Teach the Class" is an opportunity to use triangulation helpfully. Sometimes the motivation you need to shift a story or way of behaving in the world is to imagine that you're transmitting it wholesale to the next generation: Is this what you would want for them? If the answer to that is no, why would you want it for yourself? Maybe it's time to choose a new story, one that you would also choose for a daughter, a friend, or a niece.

TOOL 7: PLAYING WITH PERSONAS
Inviting All Parts of You to the Table

Personas are exaggerated portrayals of the many roles and characters we inhabit in life, different facets of ourselves that come out at different moments and under different circumstances. Persona play is rooted in the truth that while most of us tend to have a coherent sense of self and who we are, the reality is that if I were to follow you around and record how you actually show up in the world, a lot of your behaviors would likely not match your self-definition and self-concept. This isn't a problem or something to feel embarrassed about. It's just something that most humans do. We tend to fix our definition of who we are rather than acknowledging that we all have different ways of showing up, depending on the situation.

Many of our personas or parts of ourselves are protective and adaptive in their origin. While some of our personas/characters/roles are based on our innate temperament, others are constellations of behaviors that we learned early on in life from members of our family, community, and culture writ large. Sometimes personas can be helpful and needed in certain situations, especially if they are consciously deployed. However, the challenge is that personas often show up unannounced and take over as default or automated roles we play, irrespective of our current intentions, goals, and desires. The seeds of our personas are usually rooted in a core fear regarding the loss of security, approval, or control, which came under threat when we were young; the persona initially arose to help us navigate this challenging circumstance and to feel safe again. Personas also frequently serve as the channel through which unconscious stories about womanhood are passed down from generation to generation. At an early age, we observe the women in our lives inhabiting certain personas, and these characters often unconsciously serve as the backbone for our own definition of womanhood. We may conform to these roles or we may defy them; either way, we tend to be rigid in our relationship to them.

One way that we can work with the stories that we will excavate in each of the chapters about the deadly sins is to name the persona/character/part of us who shows up when we're in the grip of believing a particular story. Elise and I have provided a few examples in each chapter of personas that may resonate for you, but we encourage you to name your own as well. When we consciously bring out a persona, rather than waiting for him/her to show up uninvited, we build our capacity to become more intentional and less reactive with how we respond when we feel threatened and scared. We also soften our definition of self to include all of our various personas.

While persona work is something I first learned with the Conscious Leadership Group and then Katie Hendricks, this practice shares its underlying theory of the multifaceted self with Internal Family Systems (IFS), a type of therapy developed by psychologist Richard C. Schwartz. Just as we're describing here, the Internal Family Systems model postulates that our sense of self is actually a collection of parts, each with different needs, functions, and strategies. One goal of IFS therapy is to bring out these various parts into the open and integrate them into a unified whole. You can hear Richard Schwartz do an IFS session with Elise on an episode of her podcast *Pulling the Thread* called "Recovering Every Part of Ourselves." IFS work is typically practiced with the support of a trained therapist, while the persona work we're using here is a more playful approach that can be done solo, in a group, or with partners or friends.

If you're anything like me, I'm guessing you feel some resistance to the whole notion of parts and personas. When I was first asked to name and work with one of my personas at a Conscious Leadership Group retreat, I initially shut down and refused. In retrospect, I realize now this was fear in action. (My persona's name was Velcro, just in case you were wondering.) However, persona work has since become one of my favorite practices to use with clients, friends, teams, and myself—try to have some fun with this exercise. To play alongside you, some of our favorite personas include:

(Elise) Bag Lady Bethie: Elise's mom, Beth, went on *Donahue* when Elise was a kid to voice her very real fear of becoming a bag lady. Whenever Elise feels she's overspent on a big meal or a night out, or when she's overcommitted and needs to say no to a potentially lucrative project, the intergenerational persona Bag Lady Bethie shows up to threaten Elise with imminent homelessness if she doesn't stop spending or ceases overworking.

(Elise) Judge Judy: This persona shows up when Elise is brushing up against her unconscious envy—Judge Judy loves to point out all the ways the person in question is lacking, irritating, overreaching, falling short, or otherwise doing something that *Elise would never allow herself to do.*

(Courtney) Hillary: This persona makes a regular annual appearance around the Thanksgiving and Christmas holidays. Hillary is so focused on making sure that her family enjoys the holidays (every meal is well planned and well prepared, every gift is wrapped, and every moment of family time is spoken for with a game or activity) that she runs herself ragged. Hillary is so focused on others' fun that she ensures she has none. Hillary thinks she is living up to others' expectations of what she "has" to do, although Courtney has come to realize that the expectations that drive Hillary are her own and are largely based in fear.

(Courtney) The Girl Scout: This persona shows up whenever Courtney has to work with an expert or person of authority, particularly on behalf of her children. The Girl Scout does all her homework and research before asking for help; she is here to make sure Courtney does not look stupid and does not act like an irrational, cranky parent. The Girl Scout has earned badges in ADHD, dyslexia, asthma, breastfeeding, and tongue-tie, among many other subjects.

In each chapter, once you've named and identified your personas, there are a series of questions for you to reflect upon. Katie Hendricks may be the queen of persona play, and the questions and exercises that we've included in this section of the core process are excerpted, with some modification, from her *Centering and the Art of Intimacy Handbook: A New Psychology of Close Relationships.*

Key Takeaways from Tool 7

Personas are neither good nor bad; the goal is to use them consciously and intentionally, rather than automatically and out of fear. In addition to the inquiry process that the questions in this section of each chapter are designed to encourage, you can start working with your personas in real time, using the practices suggested below. As Katie Hendricks likes to say, "Play with your personas so that they don't play you." Suggested practices:

- Introduce your persona to people who are important to you in your life. Ask them what they appreciate about this persona and what they don't. Ask if they'd be willing to help you play and become more intentional when this part of you arises.
- If this is a practice you feel comfortable with, ask others in your life to check in with you if they suspect your persona is present. Take a breath and answer their question honestly. Check with yourself to see if this is a persona you'd intentionally like to embody.
  - If the answer is no, then shake or move your body to discard the persona and see who arises in its place.
  - If the answer is yes, then take a moment to remember what your persona really, really wants. (Refer back to your answers in the persona interview.) Collaborate with your persona to help her/him get what she/he needs.
- If there are specific situations when your persona typically shows up, get out ahead of this and either consciously invite or disinvite the persona to participate.
- When you feel yourself beginning to adopt some of your persona's signature thoughts, phrases, actions, and beliefs in real time, name that he/she is here and exaggerate his/her behaviors and thoughts. Make your persona so big that it becomes funny.

EXPANSION MOVES FOR EACH SIN

This core process is content agnostic—not only can you apply it to any and all of the sins, but you can extend it to any story you're carrying through your life, whether it fits into these containers or not. As you move from embracing goodness to wholeness, we want you to take responsibility for your relationships to the stories you have about each sin, rather than passively inheriting these cultural ideals (Tool 6), and to soften and step out of the personas you identified in Tool 7. While we have focused on using the core process as the basis for inquiry and internal discovery, there are also several practical applications of each tool that you can experiment with in everyday life (listed in the Key Takeaways sections for each tool). We hope this process becomes so embodied that you use it in all aspects of your life.

At the end of each chapter, you will find specific expansion moves for each sin, tailored to help you shift each of your stories. We have designed these expansion moves to be fun and supportive. Think of them as experiments you're conducting: What happens when you step out of your default patterns? What sensations arise in your body? What emotions come up? How do others respond? Rather than aspiring to do all the expansion moves all at once, we recommend that you pick one at a time and focus on it for several weeks. You might recruit a friend or colleague to try them with you. In addition, the expansion moves that we describe at the end of each chapter are an opportunity for you to conduct trials and safe experiments in doing something different to move yourself into the unknown; use these practices as an opportunity to explore what's possible with curiosity and openness.

1

SLOTH

Do you keep yourself running to avoid addressing your own needs?

WHAT YOU'LL RECOVER: PEACE, STILLNESS, AND THE SPACE FOR CREATIVITY

t's a story as old as time: the woman as helpmeet and devoted companion, the woman as the buttressing support for the well-being of her children and the important work of her man, the woman who "does it all" so she can "have it all"—without dropping a single ball. While our roles have evolved and changed over time, this idea of the "natural" function of a good woman hasn't really budged. We are told that essentially we are supposed to selflessly, tirelessly, and ceaselessly attend to the needs of others, whether our kids, our constituents, or our colleagues, instead of our own wants. Women are conditioned to be of service to the world, to embody the function of caregiver in all of its iterations, whether this is "being there" for our friends, being a dutiful and attentive daughter, playing the role of mother at the office, helicoptering over our children, or attending to all of our partner's emotional and physical needs—all in the course of a single day. While caretaking is core to our humanity—Who would we be without relationships with other people?—for too many women this function is extremely lopsided. With all of that "doing" for other people, it can be impossible to "do" for yourself. Not to mention, who is "doing" for you?

That last question—Who is "doing" for you?—is a big one, and the subject of a lot of books in this space. Rightly, there's a lot of cultural focus and pressure on the redistribution of work, both inside and outside the home, as so much of what women do is largely invisible, whether it's meal planning and prep, getting extra-curriculars sorted for kids, or planning an offsite work meeting. This isn't the focus of this workbook, though, if only because *you can't control other people, you can only control and change yourself.* You can try to manipulate other people's behavior to get your needs met, or you can assert your needs directly. This is big and risky—after all, what happens if someone says no?— so we'll come back to this again and again in this workbook (see Drama Triangle, page 27).

I'll give you an example. It will surprise exactly no one, particularly readers of *On Our Best Behavior,* that I've carried a lot of resentment toward my husband, Rob, over the course of our marriage. This resentment stems from the story I tell myself about everything I do for our family and for him; while he (rightly) gets credit for being a fantastic father, I don't think our effort is equitable. Historically, this has pissed me off and I've wanted him to change.

In 2022, after *On Our Best Behavior* went to print, I fell off a horse and broke my neck in two places. Miraculously, I was fine, but I learned a big lesson. For one month, I wore one of those crazy-looking neck braces and my doctor forbade me to drive, lift, bend, or do much of anything. I was quarantined to a corner of our living room couch, where I had to be present with myself for a month. I couldn't do school drop-off or pickup. I couldn't cook. I couldn't do laundry or make beds. Rob needed to pick up the slack. I could kind of type and kind of read, and I could definitely watch TV, something I hadn't historically allowed myself to do much. This made me incredibly anxious, as all of the "doing" I do in my life is largely to suppress existential anxiety about my value, which, at some level, I believe comes from being someone who does things for other people. I'm the sort of person who has taken pride in multitasking while watching (part of) a movie, who makes to-do lists after the fact so I get the satisfaction of crossing everything off. But for that month while I was in a neck brace, I had no value—or this is what I told myself. It was excruciating and scary to be present with myself while I couldn't stave off my anxiety through busyness. It was as though I'd had my blankie taken away.

I don't think this is unusual: How do you "numb" when you feel like you're not doing enough? What do you reach for and how do you self-soothe? If you're not sure, lock your phone and your computer and all your productivity tools in your car and sit with yourself for an hour. What comes up?

The other big revelation I had during my convalescence was that my husband, Rob, was not actually the person who engineered and commanded my to-do list. At no point had he ever suggested that our house be spotless, our dinners home-cooked and nutritious, our children perfectly scheduled. Once my "doing" stopped, I was left with the realization that I had manufactured those ideas myself—or more specifically, that I had subscribed wholesale to the cultural checklist of what a "good" wife and mother ought to be and do. From there, my anxiety kept me in thrall to that list. *I* was the one wielding the cattle prod, on myself—which meant I was the only one who could put it down.

Talking to women all over the world, one of the things Courtney and I hear again and again is that women do not believe that they deserve rest. While we believe our partners, our children, our co-workers, and our communities should be comfortable and cared for, we struggle to extend that care to ourselves. Many women—if not most women—feel guilty for spending time and energy on themselves, whether that's watching *Love Island,* going for a walk with a friend, or sleeping in. But when we're so busy doing, we don't have time to *be.* And when we're so busy doing, we don't let our subconscious minds come online, even though they are the source of our genius: This is why so many breakthrough thoughts can be attributed to men who were able to pursue leisurely activities and let their conscious minds rest. Einstein discovered relativity while listening to music. Steve Jobs would walk around barefoot to boost his creativity. (According to Srini Pillay, psychiatrist and Harvard professor, the conscious brain can process sixty bits per second, while the unconscious mind can process *eleven million bits per second.*) One big question for me is this: How many of us are avoiding our ultimate potential because we're too *busy* to let it become a primary driver in our lives? This is a big question. It's time to conserve your energy and create space in your life to let your true genius emerge. Here we go.

CORE PROCESS APPLIED TO THE SIN OF SLOTH

Tool 1: Is It a Fact or Is It a Story?

Excavating Unconscious Stories

For a full explanation of this tool, see page 10.

First, brainstorm some facts relevant to your relationship to work and rest. We've offered some examples below.

FACTS ABOUT SLOTH

Elise Example: I've read forty-five books in the first six months of this year; three have been for pleasure.

Courtney Example: I work thirty hours per week.

YOUR FACTS:

1. _____

2. _____

3. _____

Tip: Are these facts capable of being documented by a video recorder? For example, "I work thirty hours per week" is a fact. "I work a lot" is a story.

Second, brainstorm the stories that you make up about these facts.

STORIES I MAKE UP ABOUT SLOTH

Elise's Fact 1:

I've read forty-five books in the first six months of this year; three have been for pleasure.

Stories Elise makes up about that fact:

My life is all work and no play.

I don't have time for pleasure.

I would never allow myself to "waste time" on things that aren't productive.

Courtney's Fact 1:

I work thirty hours per week.

Stories Courtney makes up about that fact:

I don't have time to be with my friends as much as I would like.

No matter how many hours I work, I am always behind.

I can't accomplish what I want professionally without sacrificing my health.

Fact 1: _____

Stories you make up about that fact: _____

_____

_____

_____

Fact 2: _____

Stories you make up
about that fact: _____

_____

_____

Fact 3: _____

Stories you make up
about that fact: _____

_____

_____

Third, use the questions below to help you brainstorm some of the additional stories you have about sloth.

- What stories do you make up about your need for rest?
- What stories do you make up about how much you should work?
- What stories do you make up about how much mothers/daughters/wives should work?
- What stories do you make up about how much time mothers and wives should spend taking care of their families?

Elise Examples:

- It's not okay for me to relax and have fun while I still have to-dos on my list that I haven't crossed off.
- I'm the only one who can do things right; therefore I should probably do it all.
- My value as a good mother can be measured by my presence and attention in my children's lives—when I travel for work or am busy with work, my children suffer.

Courtney Examples:

- As a mom, it's my job to take care of all the administrative work associated with having kids, things like doctors' appointments, birthdays, and school paperwork.
- The value I bring to projects is my ability to work hard.
- It's important to overprepare, anticipate, and get out ahead of things that could go wrong.

YOUR STORIES:

1. _____

2. _____

3. _____

4. _____

5. _____

Now that you've excavated some of the stories that underlie your relationship to work and rest, go back through what you've written and star the two or three that drive you the most. Those are the stories that we recommend working with throughout the rest of this chapter.

While this exercise sets up the tools and exploration to come in the remainder of this chapter, it is also useful in its own right. See our explanation of Tool 1 in the "Core Process" section of the Introduction for more applications.

Tool 2: And Then What?

Tracing the Acting, Sensing, Feeling, and Thinking Loop

For a full description of this tool, see page 13.

Take the first story you want to work with from your starred list. You can repeat this process as many times as you want with different stories.

Your Story: _____

Step 1: What Actions Do You Take?

When I choose to believe this story, this is how I show up in the world:

My behaviors are: _____

I start to prioritize: _____

My attention goes to: _____

Three specific examples where I notice this story driving my behavior are:

When I: _____

_____

When I: _____

_____

When I: _____

_____

Step 2: What Sensations Do You Feel?

When I choose to believe this story, I experience the following sensations in my body:

In my forehead, I feel:

Swirling	Fogginess	Buzziness
Spaciousness	Density	Sharpness
Scattered	Throbbing	Stirred up

In the back of my neck, across my shoulders, and in my jaw, I feel:

Tight	Twisted	Pulling
Bunched	Itchy	Burning
Cord-like	Clenched	Steely
Rigid	Blocky	Prickly

Across my high chest and upper throat, I feel:

Heaviness	Constriction	Cut off
Closed in	Numb	Melting
Compressed	Achy	Pierced
Unable to breathe	Flatness	Cold

Around the stomach area, I feel:

Knotted	Fluttering	Butterflies
Nauseous	Braced	Hollow
Churning	Empty	Doubled-over

In other parts of my body, I feel:

Racing heart	Trembling hands	Low-energy
Collapsed	Wiggly	Teary
Expanded	Tingly	Stretched

These tables are adapted from Gay and Katie Hendricks's work on body sensations and intelligence. See www.hendricks.com for further information.

Step 3: What Feelings Do You Have?

When I choose to believe this story, I experience the following emotions:

Anger

LOW	MEDIUM	HIGH
Annoyed	Agitated	Enraged
Bored	Disgusted	Furious
Bothered	Frustrated	Hostile
Dissatisfied	Indignant	Livid
Irritable	Irritated	Outraged
Tense	Resentful	Vengeful

Sadness

LOW	MEDIUM	HIGH
Blue	Discouraged	Agony
Down	Gloomy	Anguished
Lonely	Hopeless	Devastated
Somber	Melancholic	Heartbroken
Solemn	Regretful	Grief-stricken
Unhappy	Sorrowful	Mourning

Fear

LOW	MEDIUM	HIGH
Concerned	Apprehensive	Frightened
Guarded	Edgy	Frozen
Hesitant	Jumpy	Panicked
Reluctant	Nervous	Petrified
Suspicious	Startled	Shocked
Vulnerable	Worried	Terrified

Joy

LOW	MEDIUM	HIGH
Calm	Cheerful	Blissful
Carefree	Excited	Delighted
Content	Graceful	Ecstatic
Lighthearted	Optimistic	Enthusiastic
Peaceful	Proud	Elated
Relaxed	Thankful	Expansive

These tables are excerpted with permission from the Conscious Leadership Group's work on emotions. See www.conscious.is for further information.

Step 4: What Thoughts Come Next?

When I choose to believe this story, the following thoughts arise:

I begin to think that: _____

I judge myself as: _____

I judge others [insert name] as: _____

_____

Tool 3: Why Stories Stick

Identifying the Underlying Fear

For a full description of this tool and the corresponding "Flavors of Fear" chart, see page 22.

Take one of the stories that you excavated in Tool 1 and explored in Tool 2. We're now going to investigate the fear activated by this particular story.

You can repeat this exercise for as many stories as you wish.

On page 57, we have included examples of this process using our own stories.

Story: _____

When I believe this story and consider the actions, body sensations, emotions, and thinking patterns that it generates, what flavor(s) of fear does it most directly map onto? You can refer to the Fight, Flee, Freeze, Fawn, and Faint box on page 25 to help you identify the sensations that you're experiencing.

- Fight
- Flee
- Freeze
- Fawn
- Faint

Tip: If this exercise feels difficult for you, you might consider standing up, repeating your story aloud a few times, and exaggerating the posture your body takes on as you go into the story.

If I were to disregard this story, what am I afraid might happen?

What am I *really* afraid might happen?

Tip: You may need to ask the question "What am I *really* afraid might happen?" a few times in order to get at the root fear that is activated. There is no wrong answer here, just an intention to understand and be with your own experience a bit more.

Does that fear seem most related to:

- A loss of control?
- A loss of approval?
- A loss of security?

As you sit with what you've learned, see if you'd be willing to acknowledge and accept that there is a part of you that feels scared. The goal is to be with this fear rather than pushing it away.

EXAMPLES:

> **Elise's Story: I'm the only one who can do things right; therefore, I should probably do it all.**

Fear Flavor: Fight

If I were to disregard this story, what am I afraid might happen?

Something important won't get done or won't get done in the right way. I could get in trouble for being remiss—for example, if I forget to order my kids' school lunch, people might think I'm a bad mom.

What am I *really* afraid might happen?

If I don't take care of everything for everyone, then I won't have any value—why would my husband stay with me if I don't take care of everything for everyone? Would he still love me if I weren't so useful?

This fear is most related to: Safety and security

> **Courtney's Story: It's important to overprepare, anticipate, and get out ahead of things that could go wrong.**

Fear Flavor: Freeze and Fawn

If I were to disregard this story, what am I afraid might happen?

I might be blamed and held accountable for anything bad that happens. I will be judged as having done a bad job.

What am I *really* afraid might happen?

The judgment and blame of others will be so strong that I could lose relationship with them.

This fear is most related to: Approval

Tool 4: Welcome to the Drama Triangle

Relating to Stories from Victimhood Consciousness

Story: _____

For a comprehensive explanation of the Drama Triangle, see page 27.

Pick a specific situation in which this story shows up in your life (see the specific examples you listed in Tool 2 for the story you're working with).

Rotate through the three positions of the Drama Triangle and answer the following questions with respect to this situation/story.

You can write your answers down in this workbook and/or use this tool as an opportunity to stand up and voice your answers out loud. Either way, this is not the time to be polite. The Victim, Villain, and Hero all see reality through overly simplified and reductionist lenses. When you take on their voices, we encourage you to use raw and simple language. Write or speak plainly. No one else is reading this material. It's here for you and you alone. We even dare you to have fun.

THE VICTIM LENS

How are you hurt, taken advantage of, or burdened?

_____

What do you find yourself worrying about over and over again?

_____

Where do you feel overwhelmed, helpless, or ineffectual?

_____

In what ways do you feel that life is unfair?

_____

THE VILLAIN LENS

Who do you blame, hold responsible, or see as the enemy?

_____

What beliefs do you have 100 percent certainty about?

_____

What/who needs to do something different to fix this situation?

_____

What do you take very seriously?

_____

THE HERO LENS

How do you ensure you are needed?

_____

Where do you take on responsibilities that are not yours?

_____

What are you avoiding or suppressing?

_____

How do you minimize or distract yourself from any discomfort?

_____

Which role in the Drama Triangle feels the most familiar to you?

_____

What are you most afraid of?

_____

What have you not yet fully faced or accepted about this situation?

_____

What truths or feelings have you not yet expressed about this situation?

_____

Tool 5: What Do These Stories Get You?

Owning the Payoffs and Costs of Our Unconscious Stories

Story: _____

Who taught me this story?

_____

What do I gain from believing this story?

_____

In what way does believing this story serve me?

_____

Who do I get to stay close with by believing this story?

_____

How do I keep this story going?

_____

If I didn't believe this story, what would I be doing instead?

_____

What does this story cost me?

_____

If I discard this story, what do I have to risk?

_____

How do I use this story to keep me from devoting my energy to that which makes me feel truly alive?

_____

In order to discard this story, what role, behavior, or way of being do I need to shed and grow out of?

_____

How would my relationship to myself change if I didn't believe this story?

_____

How would my relationship to [insert name] change if I didn't believe this story?

_____

These questions are adapted with permission from the Conscious Leadership Group's work on the Drama Triangle. See www.conscious.is for further information.

Tool 6: Teach the Class

Reclaiming Responsibility and Becoming the Creator

Story: _____

Remember: You're teaching this class at a women's college, and you want these twenty-somethings to buy into the exact same story that you are working with here. Your students need very specific instructions that they can follow to re-create and live by this story in their own lives. **The advice that you offer to your students should be actions, feelings, thoughts, and beliefs that they themselves can choose and have control over.** Really commit! Win that teaching prize!

Answer the questions that follow to help you create a game plan for your students:

What actions do you take or not take to ensure you keep believing this story?

_____

What other stories, beliefs, or thoughts should you have about yourself, others, or the world in order to keep this story going?

_____

What feelings should you repress or conceal so that this story remains the same?

_____

What do you withhold and from whom?

_____

What do you try to control that you actually can't?

_____

What do you need to believe you are right about?

_____

What agreements do you have to make and/or break with yourself or with others?

_____

What matters the most to you?

_____

What do you need to feel afraid of losing?

_____

What other "shoulds" do you need to believe?

_____

Now that you have reflected on the specific ways you have ensured that this particular story remains integral in your life, what are you willing to take responsibility for and do differently?

_____

The "Teach the Class" exercise is excerpted with permission from the Conscious Leadership Group's work on personal responsibility. See www.conscious.is for further information.

Tool 7: Playing with Personas

Inviting All Parts of You to the Table

For a full description of this tool, see page 40.

When you believe your stories about sloth, what persona shows up and dictates your way of being in the world?

EXAMPLES:

> Busy Bee Barbara: I am in a constant state of whirlwind. I have trouble relaxing because I have such a long to-do list.

> Martyr Mary: I do a lot for other people but little for myself. I'm exhausted and also sometimes resentful about that.

> I've Got This Irma: I have trouble asking for help and/or delegating, at home and at work. No one else seems to do things as well as I do.

YOUR PERSONAS:

Name and description: _____

Name and description: _____

GET TO KNOW YOUR PERSONA

Once you have a name for the persona who shows up when you believe your stories about sloth, answer the following questions:

In what situations does this persona tend to show up?

_____

What are some classic phrases this persona often says or thinks?

_____

What behaviors and actions are typical for this persona?

_____

Think of a specific situation when this persona recently showed up, and allow him/her to directly answer the following questions:

What is the most important thing to you?

_____

How do you make [insert your own name]'s life better?

_____

When did you first make your appearance?

_____

Who did you learn your style from?

_____

What are you most afraid of?

_____

What do you most want?

_____

These questions are excerpted with permission from *Centering and the Art of Intimacy Handbook,* by Gay and Katie Hendricks. See www.hendricks.com for further information.

THE PAYOFFS AND COSTS OF THIS PERSONA

When I adopt this persona,

I don't have to feel:

_____

I get to be right and make _____ wrong.

I get to control:

_____

I get to avoid:

_____

I get to feel safe by:

_____

But **when I adopt this persona,**

I don't get to try out:

_____

I don't get to enjoy:

_____

I lose the opportunity to:

_____

I lose this aspect of my humanity:

_____

These questions are adapted with permission from *Centering and the Art of Intimacy Handbook,* by Gay and Katie Hendricks. See www.hendricks.com for further information.

Expansion Moves for the Sin of Sloth

If you could wipe out the influences of your family, culture, and past and instead approach your relationship to work, rest, and play with fresh eyes, how would you act? What would you do and what would you believe? These expansion moves are designed to help you hit refresh and explore with curiosity and openness what you actually want your relationship to rest and work to be. For more on these expansion moves, see page 44.

Expansion Move 1: Persona Play as a Form of Shadow Integration

While we used persona play in Tool 7 of the core process to identify the default roles we take on with respect to womanhood, work, and rest, we can also use persona play to explore the parts of ourselves that are underdeveloped, the parts of ourselves that "we would never do," the parts of ourselves that we admire and feel attracted to in others, and conversely, the parts of ourselves that we judge and feel an aversion to when we see these parts in other people.

When you're expanding into a persona that feels foreign, scary, or "icky" to you, the practice is to deliberately take on a new character and make it as big as possible. We understand that this practice can feel, no other words to say it, scary as fuck. We promise it can be extremely powerful. If you're willing to dip your toe into this practice, we suggest following these guidelines:

- Set a defined period of time for adopting the persona, like thirty minutes after dinner.
- Give the people around you a heads-up that you're exploring a character or part of yourself that feels new or foreign to you. Explain that it's just a fun experiment and you'd like some support. If they are game to participate, name your new persona and introduce her/him and her/his defining features.
- Take this persona on and embody her/him fully. Exaggerate. Sometimes using a prop, accent, or funny voice or noise can be helpful to shift you out of your normal space. When I needed to stay off my feet for a month following a foot surgery and couldn't perform some of my normal household tasks, it was really hard and a chance to address many of my stories about usefulness, contributing, and staying busy. I created a persona named "the Reptile" and wore a lizard hat every night after dinner while I lay on the couch and rested. The lizard hat served as a reminder that I was no longer "Courtney"; I was taking on a new way of being.

After you've tried on the new persona, notice what body sensations, emotions, and thoughts come up for you. Ask others what they thought of the persona. What you learn might surprise you. For example, it turns out that the Reptile, while squirmy for me to play internally, was adored by my kids. They found her relaxed and calm. You may consider playing and exaggerating your persona a few times to see if your internal response to her/him changes over time. You may find that you grow to love her/him. While I have no intention of being the Reptile all the time, I have found that she is an essential part of myself and worthy of honoring and paying attention to.

Once this is done, you can consider whether you'd like to integrate your chosen persona into your everyday life. You can start with bite-sized doses. Perhaps this persona comes out only on weekends or during set periods of the day. You may find that people who are important in your life request that this new persona make an appearance, the way my kids wanted the Reptile to continue to make appearances after dinner so they could relax on the couch with her. With whatever persona you discover and play with, the objective of this practice is to become more conscious and intentional about the ways you're showing up in the world.

Here are some sample sloth personas we suggest you practice trying on and then make your own. If you have trouble coming up with personas in the realm of sloth, use your judgments of others to spark ideas. Who doesn't work all the time and you can't believe they get away with it? What are they doing instead?

Lazy Susan: I move languidly and slowly. Nothing is ever urgent for me. I yawn and stretch and sometimes roll around on the floor if I feel moved to. I only ever do what feels good.

Good Enough Gloria: I do the minimum to get by. I earned Cs in high school and college, and I don't give a fuck about achieving . . . shit. I don't want to waste my one wild and precious life on stupid details.

Fun Times Fiona: I'm here to have fun, duh. I have no idea what a to-do list is or the first clue as to how to make one. Why would I? I'm oblivious to whether there are dishes in the sink because doing dishes isn't fun and I only do fun things.

YOUR PERSONAS:

Name and description: _____

Name and description: _____

Expansion Move 2: End Your Complicity

Take personal responsibility for our cultural judgments of women and the onus we put on them to prioritize the care of other people—as well as the criticism we levy when we perceive women as falling short. We are just as much active creators in our culture as anyone else. Make a commitment with your friends to end the practice of gossiping about women and how much time they devote to parenting, about women who easily guard their time outside of office hours, about women who don't make being "nice" and conciliatory their primary value. If you catch yourself judging a woman, whether a celebrity, a stranger, or someone in your circle, voice the judgment out loud to yourself, then use that statement for your own learning purposes.

Expansion Move 3: Energy Audit

Rather than going about your day at seventy miles per hour, the Energy Audit is a practice that encourages you to slow down and use the sensations of your body, specifically your energy level, as a guide to whether an activity is yours to do. Here's the radical idea of this practice: Whether we like doing something, whether an activity enlivens or deadens us, whether we look forward to an activity or dread it, are important signals that many of us have lost touch with and do not trust as useful information.

The Energy Audit is an opportunity to consider these questions: "What would my life look like if I cultivated awareness of my energy levels? What would my life look like if I relied upon my energetic response to tasks to determine whether I say yes or no to them?"

In this practice, pick two to three typical days for you. Use the worksheet on page 72 to list your activities. As you devote time to each of these tasks, pay attention to whether you notice your energy rising, falling, or staying neutral. On the worksheet, note the change in your energy (you can use arrows, or a shorthand such as U for "up," D for "down," and N for "neutral"). Ideally, keep the worksheet with you throughout the day and make these notes in real time. You can also do the activity at the end of the day if that's easier.

After you've conducted your energy audit, scan for patterns. How much of your day enlivens you? How much of your day drains you? Are there recurring themes to the activities that replenish or deplete you?

For many of us, the idea of even tracking our energy is scary, and you might find yourself dipping down into the Drama Triangle with respect to this exercise and asking questions like "What's the point of tracking my energy if I can't do anything about it?" Notice any stories this exercise brings up for you and do your work. (Tools from the core process are helpful here.)

Now that you've identified some of the activities that cause your energy to fall, ask yourself if you'd be willing to change how you approach at least one of these activities. Use some of the expansion moves described on pages 73 to 76 as additional support.

If you're not willing to do anything different in your life, *great*. Then we'd like you to take personal responsibility for how you manage your energy. Going forward, anytime you spend time on an activity that drains your energy, we'd like you to say to yourself, "I'm committed to spending time on tasks that deaden me."

ENERGY AUDIT WORKSHEET

DAY 1

TASK	ENERGY LEVEL
	(Up, Down, or Neutral)

_____   _____

_____   _____

_____   _____

_____   _____

_____   _____

_____   _____

_____   _____

_____   _____

_____   _____

_____   _____

_____   _____

_____   _____

_____   _____

_____   _____

_____   _____

The Energy Audit Worksheet is adapted with permission from the Conscious Leadership Group's work on the zone of genius. See www.conscious.is for further information.

Expansion Move 4: Dump, Delegate, or Do It Differently

Also inspired by the Conscious Leadership Group, this expansion move is designed to help you think creatively about how to shift your relationship to the tasks that deplete your energy.

Look at the list of activities that cause your energy to go down and select one or two you want to work on. Option 1 is to **dump** the activity altogether. Run the experiment of letting this activity fall by the wayside and notice what happens. It's a short-term commitment so that you can learn whether an activity is really necessary after all. Perhaps the fear that has been driving you to perform the activity is never actually realized, and you now have an opportunity to rewrite the story that's in your head. For example, it turns out that my husband doesn't care that much about Father's Day. The story I had in my head, that he would be disappointed or angry if we didn't do something special to mark the day, was my own. We still often do something fun as a family on Father's Day, but I don't expend energy trying to find the perfect gift or turn it into a production.

Option 2 is to **delegate** the activity. If you became incapacitated and someone else had to take over this responsibility, who would it be? This is an opportunity to think creatively about who else might jump in. You can also delegate activities in bite-size increments: Ask your kids to make their own school lunch one day a week while you continue to take responsibility for the other four. As you delegate activities, you may find that others perform tasks differently than you do, activating your fear of loss of control. The delegation of tasks often creates an opportunity to explore this fear using the core process and learn what your control plans are costing you.

Option 3 is to do the activity **differently.** If an activity drains your energy, how might you redesign the activity so that it *brings* you energy instead? As an example, I have some old stories around writing and procrastination. (I almost did not graduate from high school, college, and law school because I missed so many deadlines.) Rather than writing portions of this workbook on our own, Elise and I scheduled deep dives where we worked side by side for two days at a time. Way more fun. Doing an activity differently is an opportunity to get creative. Sing, dance, or play music while you do the activity. Recruit a friend. Batch the activity rather than doing it daily. Redefine what success looks like. The key question to ask yourself is "How would I design this activity to ensure my energy stays up throughout its execution?"

Expansion Move 5: The No Diet

Because many of us struggle to say no, it can be easier to rely on the support of a "diet" to build this muscle. If your default response to any request is to say yes, the No Diet allows you to create and try out a new pattern. In the realm of nutrition, when you're on a diet, the point of the diet is to stop you in your tracks. Your answer to the question "Do you want dessert?" is an automatic no because, well, you're on a diet. The No Diet works the same way.

Learned through my experience with the Conscious Leadership Group, here's how the No Diet works. Commit to running the experiment for at least two weeks. Because this can be a scary exercise for many of us, it's important to remind yourself that the No Diet does not last forever. It's an experiment you're running with curiosity and openness. During these next two weeks, anytime you're asked to do something, your new default response is going to be something like "I have recently discovered that I'm a *yes*-aholic. I am actively experimenting with my ability to say yes or no, and your request has caught me during a phase where I am on a No Diet. This means that my new, default response to any request is to say no. If I change my mind and discover that I really want to do something after I've had a chance to pause, I'll let you know. But for now, my answer is a no. This is a big shift for me. Thanks for the opportunity to practice with you."

After you've said no to the new request, use some of the tools of the core process to check in with yourself. What body sensations and emotions arose when you said no? Did you notice yourself making up any stories about what might or might not happen? As you build the "no" muscle, what changes do you notice inside yourself? Do you notice your energy rising or falling? Do you notice your sense of agency changing?

With people with whom you're in daily relationship, you might find it easier to announce that you're on a No Diet rather than responding to every request. You might ask for their support in this new practice—you can also make it fun.

Ask them to catch you in the act if you forget to say no. Ask them to tempt you with irresistible asks. Come up with funny ways to say no: Sing "No, No, No" like Amy Winehouse; zip your lips like Mike Myers as Dr. Evil; or say "No, no, wouldn't be prudent," like Dana Carvey playing George H. W. Bush.

Once you've completed the No Diet, notice what the experience has been like for you and what new commitments you want to make going forward.

Expansion Move 6: Insert a Pause

The urge to say yes can be so strong for some of us that it has become automatic. This expansion practice is about actively building a pause into your response to requests. The point of the pause is to give you an opportunity to check in with yourself as to *what you really want*. Use the pause to ask yourself the following question: "As I imagine myself participating in this activity, does my energy rise or fall?" Let your energy be your guide to what you want.

Whether you use the information you glean during the pause to determine your response or whether you override these signals, you're going to learn from this process. What body sensations, emotions, and stories arise when you commit to yeses and noes that are in alignment with your energy? What body sensations, emotions, and stories arise when you don't act in alignment?

If you're working with this expansion move, it's important to note that building in a pause also requires you to commit to getting back to the person with your answer. This expansion move is not about using a pause to hope that the request magically goes away. The pause is about giving yourself time to discern what you really want. You can do this by taking physical or psychological distance (or both), running the request through your body, and then responding. Before you reflexively (and compliantly) say yes, simply ask for a minute: "Let me look at my schedule and get back to you by _____," or "I need to think about that; I'll let you know by _____." Sleep on it. Breathe through it. Then respond by the deadline that you've communicated.

Expansion Move 7: Scripts for Saying a Gentle No

Elise here. As I did this work, I noticed how excruciating I found it to say no to people, particularly in my professional life. Because I couldn't do this easily and gently, I frequently found myself in the Drama Triangle, angry with whoever had made a request that I didn't want to meet: How could they make *me* feel *bad* for asking a favor of me? They're the ones who are bad for asking in the first place! (Rinse and repeat.) I recognized that anyone could ask anything of me—this is different from compelling me to do it, clearly—and it was up to me to learn how to say a kind and firm no. There'd be no sidestepping the development of this skill. Courtney pointed me to some free scripts on the Conscious Leadership Group's website, which I workshopped until they felt like me. My typical go-to: "This sounds like an exciting opportunity and thank you for thinking of me, but I'm going to have to decline." No additional information required. We've provided some additional starters below:

- Thanks for thinking of me; I really appreciate it. While this sounds exciting, I don't have the time to participate right now. Please ask me again down the line.
- While I don't have the time to do this right now, I hope we can do something together at some point.
- Thank you for this kind offer—I've thought about it deeply but don't have a "yes" in me right now. I hope we can collaborate soon, though.
- Unfortunately, I'm tapped out with other commitments and can't take anything else on right now—thank you for thinking of me!
- I'm a bit underwater and can't say yes right now—but hopefully our calendars will align in time.
- I'd love to offer support for your project but am saying no to all incoming requests right now—thank you for asking me, though, and best of luck with your work.
- Thank you for thinking of me, but now is not the right time for me—let's touch base down the line.
- I love the work you're doing in the world and would love for this to be an easy "yes"—unfortunately, I'm too committed elsewhere. Thank you for thinking of me!
- This sounds like an amazing opportunity and important work—thank you for thinking of me. Unfortunately, I don't have the bandwidth right now.

2

ENVY

Do you know what you (actually, really) want?

WHAT YOU'LL RECOVER: ACCESS TO YOUR INNER GPS AND THE ABILITY TO GUIDE YOUR LIFE BY IT

M any years ago, I interviewed psychotherapist Lori Gottlieb about her book *Maybe You Should Talk to Someone.* During our conversation, she offered a small aside, a comment I couldn't stop thinking about. She said that she told her clients to pay attention to their envy because it showed them what they want—that the people we're envious of have something, or are doing something, that we want for ourselves. This was a huge revelation for me for two reasons. First, I had an immediate reaction to the word *envy. Ewww, no, not me. I'm not envious of anyone, ever.* I'd done enough work on myself at that point to flag that for review. Anything that inspires a big reaction is always a sign that there's good information there. The second reason made me sad: I didn't know what I wanted. At this point, I was at the height of my corporate career. I had achieved a lot, and publicly. I was married to a lovely man and had two adorable children. I owned my own house and, besides my mortgage, wasn't in debt. I was "killing it." And *yet,* I felt like I was on autopilot, pursuing a path toward a place just beyond the horizon where I would finally feel safe and secure—where I would feel good enough. On some level, I knew that this place was a fantasy. And at another level, I knew I would never get there anyway because I had no clue what I actually wanted and, in some ways, wasn't living my own life fully.

Gottlieb's comment about envy and wanting made me curious, though, and I realized that if I could actually identify my envy for what it was, if I could stop repressing it or, more frequently, *projecting* it, I could use the person sparking my envy as a divining rod for my own soul's yearning. The icky and tricky part of this process is that envy makes us feel bad: It's deeply uncomfortable to feel stirred in this way. It's so disturbing that our impulse is to get the feelings out of us, to strike out and deprecate the person who is making us feel bad. It's a nasty cycle. I believe that undiagnosed envy is the source of most woman-on-woman hate: We attack and criticize those who make us feel bad about ourselves. We rush to put them in their place. *Why her and not me?*

Courtney and I are here to ask: *Why not you?*

When the scent of envy is in the air, you'll hear things like "Who does she think she is?" or "I just don't like her," or "She rubs me the wrong way." When it gets specific, you might hear yourself saying (if you're me) things like "I didn't think her book was that good," or "Why does everyone think she's such a great interviewer?" Gross. (And specific! As you do this work, you'll notice that the women who grate your hide and the women who annoy your close friends are sometimes worlds apart.) As I started watching this envy loop in action, I started to discern that I did want things after all: I wanted to write my own book (I'd ghostwritten twelve books at that point). More specifically, I wanted to pilot my own ship and stand for myself in the world. And I started to see the women who triggered my envy as (tor)mentors: Rather than criticizing them, I studied them. They were showing me what was possible. Lacy Phillips, who runs a program called To Be Magnetic, has a name for this: She calls these people "Expanders" and recommends that people create a practice around identifying them as active models for what's possible in your own life.

All this wanting is scary, particularly in the way that envy overlaps with pride and greed. Since *On Our Best Behavior* came out, I've talked to women all over the country about their envy. I've heard how women are scared to be seen or celebrated for their gifts (pride) because they believe it will inspire envy, and they'll be destroyed. This wanting also crashes into feelings about scarcity (greed): There's an understandable belief that there's room for only one or possibly two of us to succeed, and that to get what another woman has, she must be dethroned or destroyed. We're convinced that there's not enough to go around. We'll get to our scarcity stories later in this workbook, but for now it's important to recognize that these fears are real and worthy and that they must be attended to in part because they are encouraging us all to stay small and unexpressed. It's better, we think, to believe we want nothing at all than to feel shamed for this wanting—or worse, destroyed. *Who am I to want more?* you might ask yourself. But who are you to *not express yourself fully in the world?*

I've sat in many circles of women now where I've asked them to identify—and then express—their wanting out loud. This is big, as women live the story that they don't have any wants at all. To that end, there's another rule to this game: You are not allowed to triangulate what you want through anyone else. You are not allowed to want your kids to be happy, or to want your husband to get a new, more fulfilling job, or to want your mother to finally find peace. You must limit your wanting to yourself. This simple process brings huge emotions. As we begin, you can feel the scarcity in the air, a palpable sense of anxiety that someone's want might butt up against someone else's desire. People cry as they give voice to where they feel called. As we do these circles, another quasi-miracle unfolds: *Nobody wants the same thing.* And what these women want is beautiful. "I want to pioneer a new model of regenerative farm." "I want to write a children's book about spirituality." "I want to reimagine a retirement community." "I want to start a podcast about design." "I want to open a toy store."

Before we dive into this process, one caveat: You are allowed not to like everyone. Some people are not for you, and envy might not be a factor. There are certain politicians I don't like, for example. In these cases, the women themselves mean nothing to me. I know nothing about them; I don't feel stirred by their presence. But I can point to specific behaviors and actions they've taken that I do not like and disagree with. On the other hand, if you can't identify a very specific action that a woman has taken that foments a justifiable dislike, envy is likely present, which means there's good information for you as well. Be honest with yourself: This is one of the primary ways that your soul gets your attention.

CORE PROCESS APPLIED TO THE SIN OF ENVY

Tool 1: Is It a Fact or Is It a Story?

Excavating Unconscious Stories

For a full explanation of this tool, see page 10.

First, brainstorm some facts relevant to your relationship to desire and ambition. We've offered some examples below.

FACTS ABOUT ENVY

Elise Example: I have fewer than one hundred thousand Instagram followers; there are at least five women in my space who have more than one million.

Courtney Example: I have three children and work as a coach and consultant. My dermatologist is nationally known and has six kids.

YOUR FACTS:

1. _____

2. _____

3. _____

Tip: Are these facts capable of being documented by a video recorder? For example, "I have fewer than one hundred thousand Instagram followers" is a fact. "I don't have a big enough platform to support my work" is a story.

Second, brainstorm the stories that you make up about these facts.

STORIES I MAKE UP ABOUT ENVY

Elise's Fact 1: I have fewer than one hundred thousand Instagram followers; there are at least five women in my space who have more than one million.

Stories Elise makes up about that fact: My platform should be bigger after all this time.

I don't have enough followers and will never be able to support myself as an author and podcaster.

In order to get more followers, I will have to do things I don't want to do.

Courtney's Fact 1: I have three children and work as a coach and consultant. My dermatologist is nationally known and has six kids.

Stories Courtney makes up about that fact: I don't get as much accomplished as other people.

My doctor's kids must never spend time with her.

My doctor has figured out how to balance her life in a way I haven't.

Fact 1: _____

Stories you make up about that fact: _____

_____

_____

Fact 2: _____

Stories you make up
about that fact: _____

_____

_____

Fact 3: _____

Stories you make up
about that fact: _____

_____

_____

    Third, use the questions below to help you brainstorm some of the additional stories you have about envy.

- What stories do you make up about your relationship to ambition?
- What stories do you make up about what you want and desire for your life?
- What stories do you make up about women who are ambitious?
- What stories do you make up about women who go for what they want?

Elise Examples:

- I think it's gross and unseemly when women do clickbait content on Instagram to grow their audience.
- When I see other women supporting other women who have never collaborated with me, I feel excluded.
- When I see a woman who is really successful, I convince myself that she must have a terrible home life or be an absent parent.

Courtney Examples:

- Women are judged as self-centered when they voice their ambitions.
- It's better to keep your ambitions to yourself rather than voicing them out loud, going for what you want, and risking failure.
- Knowing what you want increases conflict with others.

YOUR STORIES:

1. _____

2. _____

3. _____

4. _____

5. _____

Now that you've excavated some of the stories that underlie your relationship to wanting, ambition, and desire, go back through what you've written and star the two or three that drive you the most. Those are the stories that we recommend working with throughout the rest of this chapter.

Tool 2: And Then What?

Tracing the Acting, Sensing, Feeling, and Thinking Loop

For a full description of this tool, see page 13.

Take the first story you want to work with from your starred list. You can repeat this process as many times as you want with different stories.

Story: _____

Step 1: What Actions Do You Take?

When I choose to believe this story, this is how I show up in the world:

My behaviors are: _____

I start to prioritize: _____

My attention goes to: _____

Three specific examples where I notice this story driving my behavior are:

When I: _____

_____

When I: _____

_____

When I: _____

_____

Step 2: What Sensations Do You Feel?

When I choose to believe this story, I experience the following sensations in my body:

In my forehead, I feel:

Swirling	Fogginess	Buzziness
Spaciousness	Density	Sharpness
Scattered	Throbbing	Stirred up

In the back of my neck, across my shoulders, and in my jaw, I feel:

Tight	Twisted	Pulling
Bunched	Itchy	Burning
Cord-like	Clenched	Steely
Rigid	Blocky	Prickly

Across my high chest and upper throat, I feel:

Heaviness	Constriction	Cut off
Closed in	Numb	Melting
Compressed	Achy	Pierced
Unable to breathe	Flatness	Cold

Around the stomach area, I feel:

Knotted	Fluttering	Butterflies
Nauseous	Braced	Hollow
Churning	Empty	Doubled-over

In other parts of my body, I feel:

Racing heart	Trembling hands	Low-energy
Collapsed	Wiggly	Teary
Expanded	Tingly	Stretched

These tables are adapted from Gay and Katie Hendricks's work on body sensations and intelligence. See www.hendricks.com for further information.

Step 3: What Feelings Do You Have?

When I choose to believe this story, I experience the following emotions:

Anger

LOW	MEDIUM	HIGH
Annoyed	Agitated	Enraged
Bored	Disgusted	Furious
Bothered	Frustrated	Hostile
Dissatisfied	Indignant	Livid
Irritable	Irritated	Outraged
Tense	Resentful	Vengeful

Sadness

LOW	MEDIUM	HIGH
Blue	Discouraged	Agony
Down	Gloomy	Anguished
Lonely	Hopeless	Devastated
Somber	Melancholic	Heartbroken
Solemn	Regretful	Grief-stricken
Unhappy	Sorrowful	Mourning

Fear

LOW	MEDIUM	HIGH
Concerned	Apprehensive	Frightened
Guarded	Edgy	Frozen
Hesitant	Jumpy	Panicked
Reluctant	Nervous	Petrified
Suspicious	Startled	Shocked
Vulnerable	Worried	Terrified

Joy

LOW	MEDIUM	HIGH
Calm	Cheerful	Blissful
Carefree	Excited	Delighted
Content	Graceful	Ecstatic
Lighthearted	Optimistic	Enthusiastic
Peaceful	Proud	Elated
Relaxed	Thankful	Expansive

These tables are excerpted with permission from the Conscious Leadership Group's work on emotions. See www.conscious.is for further information.

Step 4: What Thoughts Come Next?

When I choose to believe this story, the following thoughts arise:

I begin to think that: _____

I judge myself as: _____

I judge others [insert name] as: _____

Tool 3: Why Stories Stick

Identifying the Underlying Fear

For a full description of this tool and the corresponding "Flavors of Fear" chart, see page 22.

Take one of the stories that you excavated in Tool 1 and explored in Tool 2. We're now going to investigate the fear activated by this particular story.

You can repeat this exercise for as many stories as you wish.

On pages 88 to 89, we have included examples of this process using our own stories.

Story: _____

When I believe this story and consider the actions, body sensations, emotions, and thinking patterns that it generates, what flavor(s) of fear does it most directly map onto?

- Fight
- Flee
- Freeze
- Fawn
- Faint

Tip: If this exercise feels difficult for you, you might consider standing up, repeating your story aloud a few times, and exaggerating the posture your body takes on as you go into the story.

If I were to disregard this story, what am I afraid might happen?

_____

What am I *really* afraid might happen?

_____

Tip: You may need to ask the question "What am I *really* afraid might happen?" a few times in order to get at the root fear that is activated. There is no wrong answer here, just an intention to understand and be with your own experience a bit more.

Does that fear seem most related to:

- A loss of control?
- A loss of approval?
- A loss of security?

As you sit with what you've learned, see if you'd be willing to acknowledge and accept that there is a part of you that feels scared. The goal is to be with this fear rather than pushing it away.

EXAMPLES:

Elise's Story: In order to get more followers, I would have to do things I don't want to do.

Fear Flavor: Faint

If I were to disregard this story, what am I afraid might happen?

I would be a sellout and lose my integrity.

What am I *really* afraid might happen?

If I contorted myself to please and entice followers, I'd be creating a projection of myself to meet their needs—and I would lose the ability to be myself.

This fear is most related to: Security

> **Courtney's Story: Women are judged as self-centered when they voice their ambitions.**

Fear Flavor: Fight and Faint

If I were to disregard this story, what am I afraid might happen?

If I voiced my ambitions and really went for what I want, I'd be judged as self-centered, selfish, cold, bitchy. Neither women nor men would like me.

What am I *really* afraid might happen?

I probably wouldn't get what I want anyway because others' judgments of me would be so strong. Voicing and going for my ambitions would all be for naught.

This fear is most related to: Security

Tool 4: Welcome to the Drama Triangle

Relating to Stories from Victimhood Consciousness

Story: _____

For a comprehensive explanation of the Drama Triangle, see page 27.

Pick a specific situation in which this story shows up in your life (see the specific examples you listed in Tool 2 for the story you're working with).

Rotate through the three positions of the Drama Triangle and answer the following questions with respect to this situation/story.

You can write your answers down in this workbook, use this tool as an opportunity to stand up and voice your answers out loud, or both. Either way, this is not the time to be polite. The Victim, Villain, and Hero all see reality through overly simplified and reductionist lenses. When you take on their voices, we encourage you to use raw and simple language. Write or speak plainly. No one else is reading this material. It's here for you and you alone. We even dare you to have fun.

THE VICTIM LENS

How are you hurt, taken advantage of, or burdened?

_____

What do you find yourself worrying about over and over again?

_____

Where do you feel overwhelmed, helpless, or ineffectual?

_____

In what ways do you feel that life is unfair?

_____

THE VILLAIN LENS

Who do you blame, hold responsible, or see as the enemy?

_____

What beliefs do you have 100 percent certainty about?

_____

What/who needs to do something different to fix this situation?

_____

What do you take very seriously?

_____

THE HERO LENS

How do you ensure you are needed?

_____

Where do you take on responsibilities that are not yours?

_____

What are you avoiding or suppressing?

_____

How do you minimize or distract yourself from any discomfort?

_____

REFLECTION

Which role in the Drama Triangle feels the most familiar to you?

_____

What are you most afraid of?

_____

What have you not yet fully faced or accepted about this situation?

_____

What truths or feelings have you not yet expressed about this situation?

_____

Tool 5: What Do These Stories Get You?

Owning the Payoffs and Costs of Our Unconscious Stories

Story: _____

Who taught me this story?

_____

What do I gain from believing this story?

_____

In what way does believing this story serve me?

_____

Who do I get to stay close with by believing this story?

_____

How do I keep this story going?

_____

If I didn't believe this story, what would I be doing instead?

_____

What does this story cost me?

_____

If I discard this story, what do I have to risk?

_____

How do I use this story to keep me from devoting my energy to that which makes me feel truly alive?

_____

In order to discard this story, what role, behavior, or way of being do I need to shed and grow out of?

_____

How would my relationship to myself change if I didn't believe this story?

_____

How would my relationship to [insert name] change if I didn't believe this story?

_____

These questions are adapted with permission from the Conscious Leadership Group's work on the Drama Triangle. See www.conscious.is for further information.

Tool 6: Teach the Class
Reclaiming Responsibility and Becoming the Creator

Story: _____

Remember: You're teaching this class at a women's college, and you want these twenty-somethings to buy into the exact same story that you are working with here. Your students need very specific instructions that they can follow to re-create and live by this story in their own lives. **The advice that you offer to your students should be actions, feelings, thoughts, and beliefs that they themselves can choose and have control over.** Really commit! Win that teaching prize!

Answer the questions that follow to help you create a game plan for your students:

What actions do you take or not take to ensure you keep believing this story?

_____

What other stories, beliefs, or thoughts should you have about yourself, others, or the world in order to keep this story going?

_____

What feelings should you repress or conceal so that this story remains the same?

_____

What do you withhold and from whom?

_____

What do you try to control that you actually can't?

_____

What do you need to believe you are right about?

_____

What agreements do you have to make and/or break with yourself or with others?

_____

What matters the most to you?

_____

What do you need to feel afraid of losing?

_____

What other "shoulds" do you need to believe?

_____

Now that you have reflected on the specific ways you have ensured that this particular story remains integral in your life, what are you willing to take responsibility for and do differently?

_____

The "Teach the Class" exercise is excerpted with permission from the Conscious Leadership Group's work on personal responsibility. See www.conscious.is for further information.

Tool 7: Playing with Personas

Inviting All Parts of You to the Table

For a full description of this tool, see page 40.

When you believe the stories you have about envy, what persona shows up and dictates your way of being in the world?

EXAMPLES:

> Ambition Police Amber: I judge other women for naming and unabashedly going after their wants, goals, and desires.

> Frau Schadenfreude: I'm secretly (or not so secretly) relieved when it's revealed that a woman who seems to have it all is actually suffering or not what she seems.

> I'm Good Gloria: I don't articulate my wants, goals, and desires. I find a way to be content with what I've got.

YOUR PERSONAS:

Name and description: _____

Name and description: _____

GET TO KNOW YOUR PERSONA

Once you have a name for the persona who shows up when you believe your stories about envy, answer the following questions:

In what situations does this persona tend to show up?

_____

What are some classic phrases this persona often says or thinks?

_____

What behaviors and actions are typical for this persona?

_____

Think of a specific situation when this persona recently showed up, and allow him/her to directly answer the following questions:

What is the most important thing to you?

_____

How do you make [insert your own name]'s life better?

_____

When did you first make your appearance?

_____

Who did you learn your style from?

_____

What are you most afraid of?

_____

What do you most want?

_____

These questions are excerpted with permission from *Centering and the Art of Intimacy Handbook*, by Gay and Katie Hendricks. See www.hendricks.com for further information.

THE PAYOFFS AND COSTS OF THIS PERSONA

When I adopt this persona,

I don't have to feel:

_____

I get to be right and make _____ wrong.

I get to control:

_____

I get to avoid:

_____

I get to feel safe by:

_____

But **when I adopt this persona,**

I don't get to try out:

_____

I don't get to enjoy:

_____

I lose the opportunity to:

_____

I lose this aspect of my humanity:

_____

These questions are adapted with permission from *Centering and the Art of Intimacy Handbook,* by Gay and Katie Hendricks. See www.hendricks.com for further information.

Expansion Moves for the Sin of Envy

If you could wipe away the influences of your family, culture, and past and instead approach your relationship to ambition, wanting, and desire with fresh eyes, how would you act? What would you do and what would you believe? These expansion moves are designed to help you hit refresh and explore with curiosity and openness what you *actually* want your relationship to envy to be—and how it can lead you to your full self. For more on these expansion moves, see page 44.

Expansion Move 1: Reclaim the Gift of Envy

Rather than thinking of *envy* as a dirty word, make a pact with a few friends to reframe envy as a useful tool for pointing you in the direction of what you want. With these friends, commit to becoming alert and hypercurious to anytime any of you notice envy. Rather than suppressing the body sensations, emotions, and thoughts that typically accompany envy, out your envy so that you can use it to see what matters to you. The practice will look something like "Hey, I just noticed a twinge of envy arise in me as you talked about your vacation. Thank you for helping me discover that I'm wanting my own downtime."

With these friends, you can also have a regular envy check-in practice. Whenever you meet up, reserve a few minutes at the beginning of your conversation to look for and out your envies. The key here is to assume that envy is arising in us all the time. Because we've made envy something to be ashamed of rather than a gift, we have a habit of stuffing it down rather than using it as a tool for self-discovery.

When doing the envy practice, it can be hard to figure out what deeper want a particular envy is pointing to. If that's the case for you, make sure you voice the envy out loud. Then pause and give yourself time to wonder with curiosity and without judgment. Give yourself time for an answer to emerge rather than needing it to happen right away. For example, I notice that I sometimes feel envy toward friends of mine who don't have children. But if I sit for a moment with that envy and keep asking what I really want, I see that I want more opportunity for spontaneity in my life, more opportunity to say yes without having to plan for and anticipate all the logistical consequences. Once I identify this deeper want, I can start looking for how I can take responsibility to meet this need, with or without children. One tip: Look for a shift in the energy of your body (usually a simultaneous feeling of your heart and energy rising while your body also feels settled and grounded) as a clue that you've hit on a deeper want that matters to you.

Expansion Move 2: Judgment as Projection

Often we judge others because they're daring to do the thing we would never do, or they're daring to do something we don't think we could get away with. Therefore, anytime you catch yourself judging someone else, whether it's a celebrity or someone closer to home, the judgment points to a shadow part of yourself that you have disowned or that you believe you have to disown. This is what we mean by the concept of projection.

Therefore, judgments become opportunities for us to again discover what we want but think isn't possible. You can put this expansion move into practice as judgments spontaneously arise, or you can proactively make a list of people you irrationally (or rationally) dislike. In either case, notice the specific qualities or characteristics that bother you. If you're doing this exercise proactively, you can even make it big and fun and do it as a Burn Book, à la *Mean Girls*. As you notice the qualities that you find yourself judging, ask yourself the following questions:

- What does this person have or do that, if I'm really, really honest, I'd like a little bit (or a lot) of too?
- What is this person getting away with that I believe I can't?
- What "rule" has he or she broken that I feel like I have to follow?
- If I didn't have to worry about what might happen or what others might think, what does this person have or do that I want also?

Expansion Move 3: End Your Complicity

Take personal responsibility for our cultural judgments of women and ambition. We are just as much active creators in our culture as anyone else. Make a commitment with your friends to end the practice of gossiping about women who go after what they want; who seem to have accomplished a lot; or who are brazen in their ambitions, goals, and desires. If you catch yourself judging a woman, whether a celebrity, a stranger, or someone in your circle, voice the judgment out loud and use it for your own learning purposes.

When you notice a friend or colleague voicing their wishes or wants, thank them for their honesty and clarity and ask for even more information. Desires are an expression of what matters to us and what we long for. Tell your friends and colleagues how much closer you feel to them because they have fully expressed their wants. Notice if the expression of others' wants triggers stories within you, such as "It's my job to do something about this" or "There's no way we can both get what we want," and use tools from the core process to learn and grow from these stories.

Expansion Move 4: The Gift of Complaining

Inside every complaint is a want. Rather than either suppressing your complaints or venting as a form of reactivity, transform complaints into an opportunity to discover what you want and what matters to you.

When you notice yourself becoming irritated about something and/or starting to complain (either as a voice inside your head or out loud), stop and make the complaining intentional. Grab a friend or someone who is willing to listen and explain the following: "One thing I have learned about myself is that complaining helps me discover what I want. Would you mind holding space for me so that I can be deliberate about my complaining? I want to emphasize that the point of my complaining is not for you to do anything differently or for you to help me solve or fix the issue. The point of the complaining is that it is a tool for my own self-discovery and learning."

If no one is around and you need to do this on your own, that's okay too. Keep these instructions in mind.

Once you've set up your complaining container, allow yourself to fully go for it. Complain. Ask yourself what's bothering you. Ask yourself what you don't like. Ask yourself what irritates you or what you find deficient. If you're someone who likes to get carried away with your complaining (for example, Courtney!), then we recommend that you set a timer for two minutes and limit this practice.

After you've had a chance to complain, have your partner ask you the following questions (or ask them of yourself). Sit with the question and repeat it to yourself again and again until an answer arises.

- What do these complaints tell you that you want?
- What is the deeper want underneath the first want?
- What is one step *you* can take in service of this desire?

Expansion Move 5: Unabashedly Wanting

In the workshops we've done together, we've noticed a funny thing: Women struggle to say "I want" and often choose to say "I would like" instead. Many of us are uncomfortable asserting our desires in a straightforward way—without finding an object or person to triangulate our wanting through. Practice saying "I want" as much as possible, in a simple and unadorned way. Practice at work: "I want to meet with you at the end of the day." Practice at restaurants: "I want the chicken paillard." (We know, we know, *I would like.*) Practice with your partner: "I want to go to bed at 9 p.m. I want you to rub my feet."

To grow your ease with articulating what you want, a fun practice that we use is saying "I want" out loud, four or five times, in the following different vocal tones and intensities:

- In the voice of a queen who gets what she wants
- In the voice of a whiny toddler
- Using your sexiest whisper
- In the voice of a drill sergeant
- While throwing a temper tantrum
- In the voice of a no-nonsense boss
- As Mary Poppins
- As an evangelist preacher

Notice what comes up in you—your body sensations, emotions, and thoughts—as you try these voices on. They might invoke big feelings for you, particularly if you were shut down as a child for having tantrums or felt bossed around by authority figures. That's okay; simply stay present and notice what happens. You might want to incorporate one of these voices into your everyday life to help build your "unabashedly wanting" muscle.

For extra credit, you can also get your body involved. Think of something you know and like, and imagine that it's in front of you. It could be an ice-cream sundae, your child with outstretched arms, a cozy sweater. Close your eyes and say "I want" as you reach for it. Pause for several seconds and notice what's present in your body. Next, think of something you really dislike and imagine that it's in front of you. Close your eyes and say "I want" as you reach out for it. Pause and notice what's present. Can you feel the difference? Going forward, practice sensing into your body to see what it wants as well.

Expansion Move 6: Make Yourself Blush

Courtney here. Many of us suppress or "right-size" our desires for fear that our wants can't be met, that we're asking for too much, or that we think too highly of ourselves. The silencing effect of these fears then becomes self-fulfilling; our failure to articulate what we want means we're unlikely to ever get it. My teacher and friend Diana Chapman has taught me that if I'm not blushing or squirming when I imagine what I want, then I'm not wanting big enough. Questions you can use to induce blushing are:

- If money/time/others' needs were not a constraint, what would I really, really want?
- If I didn't worry about what others might think of me, the likelihood of success, or the feasibility of achieving my goal, what would I really, really want?
- If I were to dream twice as big as I typically allow myself, what would I desire?
- What secret want of mine am I too scared to voice out loud?

You can ask yourself these questions about your most important relationships, your professional aspirations, your health, how you spend your time, the daily rhythms of your life, or any other area where you feel dissatisfaction or a longing for something more.

You don't have to articulate these big desires to everyone, but cultivate a practice of devoting some time—either on your own or with a few key confidants—to wanting what seems impossible. Whether you get exactly what you want is not the point. Daring to articulate what we want at the big and blushing level ensures that we know where we really want to go, that we align our time and resources accordingly, and that any stories or fears we may have learned about what's possible do not become self-limiting.

3

PRIDE

Are you capable of celebrating yourself?
(Birthdays don't count.)

WHAT YOU'LL RECOVER: ACCESS TO THE FULL EXPRESSION AND HONORING OF YOUR GIFTS

As readers of *On Our Best Behavior* might remember, I was a high-achieving child. I used to tell myself that this was my parents' fault, since clearly their love must have been conditioned to the number of trophies that I won. But then I remembered that my parents actually sent me to a school that didn't give grades, tests, or textbooks. I found work-arounds to this, though, and pursued any avenue to distinguish myself. I was convinced that safety and security lived on the other side of making it to the National MATHCOUNTS competition (yep, I was a mathlete)[*] or training to be an Olympic freestyle skier (no dice).

There was a key condition to all this achievement, though: I would need to distinguish myself *quietly*. My parents were insistent that I not draw attention to myself. *Be humble. Don't get a big head. Nobody likes a braggart.* The key word in that last phrase is *like*. It's critical for women and girls to remain likable—to be unthreatening, compliant, small, and forever connected to and embedded in the group. This connection is won by never standing apart and never distinguishing or individuating yourself fully. We all know what happens to the tall poppy in the poppy field: It loses its head.

[*] Courtney was *also* a MATHCOUNTS mathlete.

I imbibed this messaging fully. Be excellent, but don't draw attention to your-self in the process. By extension, don't seek attention or affirmation. If someone compliments you, defer, demur, deflect, or find someone else to credit for your achievement. Women are typically black belts when it comes to deflection—we know this story all too well. Do any of these sentence starters sound familiar? "It's really not a big deal, I . . ."; "I wouldn't be anything without . . ."; "I'm really just okay, you should see . . ."; "I may be decent at this, but I'm terrible at . . ."

This experience of excelling and hiding is not unique to me. After all, girls and women are excellent: We've been outperforming boys and men in school for a century. But you wouldn't know it because we don't flex our achievements, nor are we largely recognized for them (cue "Manels," i.e., the panels composed solely of men, which I've written about extensively on my Substack). Women know better than to play big or seek recognition. For one, it's dangerous. Col-lectively, we can tolerate only so much visibility for a woman before we rush to put her in her place. For easy slam-dunk examples, look no further than female celebrities, musicians, and founders. I wrote about this extensively in *On Our Best Behavior*, but my guess is that you can list at least ten such women in under sixty seconds, women all ceremoniously destroyed or canceled because we decided they'd had enough attention. We'll be there for their comeback tours, though, and we'll buy all the merch. #FreeBritney.

We might proclaim that this happens only to famous women—or women who "deserve" it—but it's a playbook for all of us, and for our daughters too. To protect against this possibility, the rest of us train to stay small. It doesn't need to be a conscious decision for this to be real. But the more we minimize ourselves and our achievements, the less permission we give to other women to stand tall. There *is* safety in numbers—it's never great to be the only one—so it's incumbent on all of us to shine our lights brightly. As women, we instinctively know that the light is safer than the darkness, yet we've been conditioned to believe that it's bet-ter to stay in the shadows.

One of the points Courtney makes about why she's particularly passionate about coaching women in groups is that we need practice individuating while staying in community. We need to both understand and experience that this is possible. This stems from the work of the legendary professor Carol Gilligan, the first developmental psychologist to study the ways girls come to understand their place in the world. Gilligan's research posits that it is through a *cultural process*—again, not natural—that girls come to see themselves as *in service* to the world, while boys see themselves as *in* the world. Girls see their roles as relational, while boys see themselves as separate, through the process of individuation and growth. Gilligan's point is that psychological development is not actually gendered in the way we've insisted in our society; it's *human*. We must individuate and grow *and* integrate this growth into relationships and care. I bring up Gilligan because too many boys and men are stuck in individualism and separation overdrive, while too many girls and women are scared to risk relationship in the quest to fully develop themselves.

The world is increasingly scary and uncertain—like our boys and men, it can't keep pace with our hyperindividualistic culture. In our experience, women understand this and are loath to participate in the wider culture if it will only perpetuate these problems. Many women, particularly women who have the financial means because they've ascended the corporate ranks, are dropping out because they sense an increasing dissonance between their values and the values of the world. But we can't let this happen: We need women to engage fully, just as they are. We must all bring our gifts to bear, in whatever space or sphere we're called to.

We must make it safer for women to do this, in part by watching our own tendencies to police other women for being "too big for their britches." We must resist the urge to "put women back in their place." This is instinctive and fierce, and many of us aren't even conscious that we're doing it: It is a story. I watch myself carefully now, specifically for the instinct to swat another woman down. I even practice "Exposure Therapy," where I listen to women brag. It makes me *so uncomfortable,* which is precisely the point—we need to allow women to flex their capacities in the same way we allow men. For me, it's exposure therapy to listen to *Pivot* with Kara Swisher and Scott Galloway, a podcast that I love: Kara *flexes,* as much as if not more than Scott, and it makes me squirm, which is how I know it's good for me to listen closely as she shows women there's another way. Kara is living her gifts, or fulfilling her purpose, though that word is tough.

The idea of "purpose" is overused and ill-defined—it's also, paradoxically, both overwhelming and limited. It suggests that we're each here to fulfill one specific role: that you should know your purpose and do it. Courtney and I think of purpose, or potential, as an emergent quality: It is something that shifts and evolves over time, that will never be fully realized. It's not an achievement; it's a process of ongoing contribution to the world. It's also hard to recognize in the present: Often you won't see what you've been up to until it's in the past, a bit like studying the wake from a speedboat to ascertain the path taken through the water. You won't know the value of what you're creating in this moment until it's done.

To that end, it can be hard to ascertain your gifts if you're not in motion—it's a bit like a game of call and response, or Marco Polo. Only after you begin to express yourself can you sense whether you are bringing these gifts to fruition—both in the way you're received and in your own soul. Is there resonance? Does your life feel like a full-body yes? Let's find out.

CORE PROCESS APPLIED TO THE SIN OF PRIDE
Tool 1: Is It a Fact or Is It a Story?
Excavating Unconscious Stories

For a full explanation of this tool, see page 10.

First, brainstorm some facts relevant to your relationship to desire and ambition. We've offered some examples below.

FACTS ABOUT PRIDE

Elise Example: I won the Henley Regatta in high school.

Courtney Example: I have two graduate degrees, one from Yale and one from NYU.

YOUR FACTS:

1. _____

2. _____

3. _____

Tip: Are these facts capable of being documented by a video recorder? For example, "I have two graduate degrees, one from Yale and one from NYU" is a fact. "I'm really smart" is a story.

Second, brainstorm the stories that you make up about these facts.

STORIES I MAKE UP ABOUT PRIDE

Elise's Fact 1:

I won the Henley Regatta in high school.

Stories Elise makes up about that fact:

Rowing is a team sport; it doesn't mean that much individually.

I abandoned rowing—even though I really liked it—because the coaches wanted me to gain thirty pounds in college and I was too vain.

I actually hate direct competition—even though I'm really competitive.

Courtney's Fact 1:

I have two graduate degrees, one from Yale and one from NYU.

Stories Courtney makes up about that fact:

It's not that big of a deal where I went to graduate school. I don't use anything I learned getting those degrees anyway.

Even though I went to Yale Law School, I was never that great at being a lawyer.

Telling people where I went to graduate school creates expectations that make me uncomfortable.

Fact 1: _____

Stories you make up about that fact: _____

_____

_____

Fact 2: _____

Stories you make up about that fact: _____

_____

_____

Fact 3: _____

Stories you make up about that fact: _____

_____

_____

Third, use the questions below to help you brainstorm some of the additional stories you have about pride.

- What stories do you make up about what you have accomplished so far in your life?
- What stories do you make up about sharing and celebrating your accomplishments with others?
- What stories do you make up about women who celebrate their natural talents and accomplishments?
- What stories do you make up about women shining as brightly as possible?

Elise Examples:

- I typically have a visceral reaction when women post glamorous moments from their life on social media. If they're not making gentle fun of their partners, teaching me something, or being funny in general, I don't want to see it.
- It's cool when people brag about you; less cool when you brag about yourself.
- If I draw too much attention to myself, I'll inspire envy, and I will be destroyed.

Courtney Examples:

- It would make others uncomfortable if I fully celebrated and shared all I have achieved.
- Doing a good job and getting great feedback just raises the performance bar for next time.
- Given my age, I should have achieved more than I already have.

YOUR STORIES:

1. _____

2. _____

3. _____

4. _____

5. _____

Now that you've excavated some of the stories that underlie your relationship to being seen and celebrated, go back through what you've written and star the two or three that drive you the most. Those are the stories that we recommend working with throughout the rest of this chapter.

Tool 2: And Then What?

Tracing the Acting, Sensing, Feeling, and Thinking Loop

For a full description of this tool, see page 13.

Take the first story you want to work with from your starred list. You can repeat this process as many times as you want with different stories.

Story: _____

Step 1: What Actions Do You Take?

When I choose to believe this story, this is how I show up in the world:

My behaviors are: _____

I start to prioritize: _____

My attention goes to: _____

Three specific examples where I notice this story driving my behavior are:

When I: _____

When I: _____

When I: _____

Step 2: What Sensations Do You Feel?

When I choose to believe this story, I experience the following sensations in my body:

In my forehead, I feel:

Swirling	Fogginess	Buzziness
Spaciousness	Density	Sharpness
Scattered	Throbbing	Stirred up

In the back of my neck, across my shoulders, and in my jaw, I feel:

Tight	Twisted	Pulling
Bunched	Itchy	Burning
Cord-like	Clenched	Steely
Rigid	Blocky	Prickly

Across my high chest and upper throat, I feel:

Heaviness	Constriction	Cut off
Closed in	Numb	Melting
Compressed	Achy	Pierced
Unable to breathe	Flatness	Cold

Around the stomach area, I feel:

Knotted	Fluttering	Butterflies
Nauseous	Braced	Hollow
Churning	Empty	Doubled-over

In other parts of my body, I feel:

Racing heart	Trembling hands	Low-energy
Collapsed	Wiggly	Teary
Expanded	Tingly	Stretched

These tables are adapted from Gay and Katie Hendricks's work on body sensations and intelligence. See www.hendricks.com for further information.

Step 3: What Feelings Do You Have?

When I choose to believe this story, I experience the following emotions:

Anger

LOW	MEDIUM	HIGH
Annoyed	Agitated	Enraged
Bored	Disgusted	Furious
Bothered	Frustrated	Hostile
Dissatisfied	Indignant	Livid
Irritable	Irritated	Outraged
Tense	Resentful	Vengeful

Sadness

LOW	MEDIUM	HIGH
Blue	Discouraged	Agony
Down	Gloomy	Anguished
Lonely	Hopeless	Devastated
Somber	Melancholic	Heartbroken
Solemn	Regretful	Grief-stricken
Unhappy	Sorrowful	Mourning

Fear

LOW	MEDIUM	HIGH
Concerned	Apprehensive	Frightened
Guarded	Edgy	Frozen
Hesitant	Jumpy	Panicked
Reluctant	Nervous	Petrified
Suspicious	Startled	Shocked
Vulnerable	Worried	Terrified

Joy

LOW	MEDIUM	HIGH
Calm	Cheerful	Blissful
Carefree	Excited	Delighted
Content	Graceful	Ecstatic
Lighthearted	Optimistic	Enthusiastic
Peaceful	Proud	Elated
Relaxed	Thankful	Expansive

These tables are excerpted with permission from the Conscious Leadership Group's work on emotions. See www.conscious.is for further information.

Step 4: What Thoughts Come Next?

When I choose to believe this story, the following thoughts arise:

I begin to think that:_____

I judge myself as: _____

I judge others [insert name] as: _____

Tool 3: Why Stories Stick

Identifying the Underlying Fear

For a full description of this tool and the corresponding "Flavors of Fear" chart, see page 22.

Take one of the stories that you excavated in Tool 1 and explored in Tool 2. We're now going to investigate the fear activated by this particular story.

You can repeat this exercise for as many stories as you wish.

On page 118, we have included examples of this process using our own stories.

Story: _____

When I believe this story and consider the actions, body sensations, emotions, and thinking patterns that it generates, what flavor(s) of fear does it most directly map onto?

- Fight
- Flee
- Freeze
- Fawn
- Faint

Tip: If this exercise feels difficult for you, you might consider standing up, repeating your story aloud a few times, and exaggerating the posture your body takes on as you go into the story.

If I were to disregard this story, what am I afraid might happen?

_____

What am I *really* afraid might happen?

_____

Tip: You may need to ask the question "What am I *really* afraid might happen?" a few times in order to get at the root fear that is activated. There is no wrong answer here, just an intention to understand and be with your own experience a bit more.

Does that fear seem most related to:

- A loss of control?
- A loss of approval?
- A loss of security?

As you sit with what you've learned, see if you'd be willing to acknowledge and accept that there is a part of you that feels scared. The goal is to be with this fear rather than pushing it away.

EXAMPLES:

> **Elise's Story: If I draw too much attention to myself, I'll inspire envy and I will be destroyed.**

Fear Flavor: Freeze and Fawn

If I were to disregard this story, what am I afraid might happen?

Should my platform get too much bigger, people will think I have a big head—they'll begin looking for ways to criticize me and tear me down. I need to remain hypervigilant about my likability and relatability factor.

What am I *really* afraid might happen?

I'll be canceled and destroyed and will not be able to support my family.

This fear is most related to: Security

> **Courtney's Story: Telling people where I went to graduate school creates expectations that make me uncomfortable.**

Fear Flavor: Freeze

If I were to disregard this story, what am I afraid might happen?

People might expect more from me than I can deliver. People start relating to me only as a brain. I might have to have all the answers.

What am I *really* afraid might happen?

People will judge me as inadequate.

This fear is most related to: Approval

Tool 4: Welcome to the Drama Triangle

Relating to Stories from Victimhood Consciousness

Story: _____

For a comprehensive explanation of the Drama Triangle, see page 27.

Pick a specific situation in which this story shows up in your life (see the specific examples you listed in Tool 2 for the story you're working with).

Rotate through the three positions of the Drama Triangle and answer the following questions with respect to this situation/story.

You can write your answers down in this workbook and/or use this tool as an opportunity to stand up and voice your answers out loud. Either way, this is not the time to be polite. The Victim, Villain, and Hero all see reality through overly simplified and reductionist lenses. When you take on their voices, we encourage you to use raw and simple language. Write or speak plainly. No one else is reading this material. It's here for you and you alone. We even dare you to have fun.

THE VICTIM LENS

How are you hurt, taken advantage of, or burdened?

_____

What do you find yourself worrying about over and over again?

_____

Where do you feel overwhelmed, helpless, or ineffectual?

_____

In what ways do you feel that life is unfair?

_____

THE VILLAIN LENS

Who do you blame, hold responsible, or see as the enemy?

_____

What beliefs do you have 100 percent certainty about?

_____

What/who needs to do something different to fix this situation?

_____

What do you take very seriously?

_____

THE HERO LENS

How do you ensure you are needed?

_____

Where do you take on responsibilities that are not yours?

_____

What are you avoiding or suppressing?

_____

How do you minimize or distract yourself from any discomfort?

_____

REFLECTION

Which role in the Drama Triangle feels the most familiar to you?

_____

What are you most afraid of?

_____

What have you not yet fully faced or accepted about this situation?

_____

What truths or feelings have you not yet expressed about this situation?

_____

Tool 5: What Do These Stories Get You?
Owning the Payoffs and Costs of Our Unconscious Stories

Story: _____

Who taught me this story?

_____

What do I gain from believing this story?

_____

In what way does believing this story serve me?

_____

Who do I get to stay close with by believing this story?

_____

How do I keep this story going?

_____

If I didn't believe this story, what would I be doing instead?

_____

What does this story cost me?

_____

If I discard this story, what do I have to risk?

_____

How do I use this story to keep me from devoting my energy to that which makes me feel truly alive?

_____

In order to discard this story, what role, behavior, or way of being do I need to shed and grow out of?

_____

How would my relationship to myself change if I didn't believe this story?

_____

How would my relationship to [insert name] change if I didn't believe this story?

_____

These questions are adapted with permission from the Conscious Leadership Group's work on the Drama Triangle. See www.conscious.is for further information.

Tool 6: Teach the Class
Reclaiming Responsibility and Becoming the Creator

Story: _____

Remember: You're teaching this class at a women's college, and you want these twenty-somethings to buy into the exact same story that you are working with here. Your students need very specific instructions that they can follow to re-create and live by this story in their own lives. **The advice that you offer to your students should be actions, feelings, thoughts, and beliefs that they themselves can choose and have control over.** Really commit! Win that teaching prize!

Answer the questions that follow to help you create a game plan for your students:

What actions do you take or not take to ensure you keep believing this story?

_____

What other stories, beliefs, or thoughts should you have about yourself, others, or the world in order to keep this story going?

_____

What feelings should you repress or conceal so that this story remains the same?

_____

What do you withhold and from whom?

_____

What do you try to control that you actually can't?

_____

What do you need to believe you are right about?

_____

What agreements do you have to make and/or break with yourself or with others?

_____

What matters the most to you?

_____

What do you need to feel afraid of losing?

_____

What other "shoulds" do you need to believe?

_____

Now that you have reflected on the specific ways you have ensured that this particular story remains integral in your life, what are you willing to take responsibility for and do differently?

_____

The "Teach the Class" exercise is excerpted with permission from the Conscious Leadership Group's work on personal responsibility. See www.conscious.is for further information.

Tool 7: Playing with Personas

Inviting All Parts of You to the Table

For a full description of this tool, see page 40.

When you believe the stories you have about pride, what persona shows up and dictates your way of being in the world?

EXAMPLES:

Anti-Narcissist Nancy: I don't think what I do is that special. I wouldn't want a big head or a big ego to get the best of me.

Humble Holly: I don't talk that much about my talents. No bragging allowed, duh!

Crowd Pleaser Clarice: I minimize my talents and overly give credit to others so that I don't stand out. I don't want to risk disconnection with my friends, colleagues, or family.

YOUR PERSONAS:

Name and description: _____

Name and description: _____

GET TO KNOW YOUR PERSONA

Once you have a name for the persona who shows up when you believe your stories about pride, answer the following questions:

In what situations does this persona tend to show up?

_____

What are some classic phrases this persona often says or thinks?

_____

What behaviors and actions are typical for this persona?

_____

Think of a specific situation when this persona recently showed up, and allow him/her to directly answer the following questions:

What is the most important thing to you?

_____

How do you make [insert your own name]'s life better?

_____

When did you first make your appearance?

_____

Who did you learn your style from?

_____

What are you most afraid of?

_____

What do you most want?

_____

These questions are excerpted with permission from *Centering and the Art of Intimacy Handbook*, by Gay and Katie Hendricks. See www.hendricks.com for further information.

THE PAYOFFS AND COSTS OF THIS PERSONA

When I adopt this persona,

I don't have to feel:

_____

I get to be right and make _____ wrong.

I get to control:

_____

I get to avoid:

_____

I get to feel safe by:

_____

But when I adopt this persona,

I don't get to try out:

_____

I don't get to enjoy:

_____

I lose the opportunity to:

_____

I lose this aspect of my humanity:

_____

These questions are adapted with permission from *Centering and the Art of Intimacy Handbook,* by Gay and Katie Hendricks. See www.hendricks.com for further information.

Expansion Moves for the Sin of Pride

If you could wipe out the influences of your family, culture, and past, and instead approach your relationship to appreciation, attention, and the expression of your gifts with fresh eyes, how would you act? What would you do and what would you believe? These expansion moves are designed to help you hit refresh and explore with curiosity and openness what you actually want your relationship to pride to be. For more on these expansion moves, see page 44.

Expansion Move 1: End the Bragging Police

Take personal responsibility for our cultural judgments of women who are self-confident and feel comfortable speaking about their achievements, skills, and expertise. We are just as much active creators in our culture as anyone else. Make a commitment with your friends to end the practice of gossiping about women who share their achievements with the world or who are making visible waves in their industries. If you catch yourself judging or criticizing a woman for being "too big for her britches," whether a celebrity, a stranger, or someone in your circle, voice the judgment out loud and use it for your own learning purposes. Are you committed to supporting women appreciating themselves or not? This is a chance to practice and live your commitment.

Expansion Move 2: Capability Journal

We're all familiar with the concept of a gratitude journal, but we believe that many women would benefit from keeping a "capability journal" instead. It's a pretty simple practice: Create a practice of listing three things that went well that day or that happened smoothly or without a lot of fuss for you. As a next step, reflect on the actions, skills, or talents you brought to those moments to ensure their success. Many of us tend to focus on what went poorly or what could have gone better rather than what went well; the practice of keeping a capability journal intentionally flips that bias. Also, many of us take for granted what comes easily to us, or we tend to ascribe success to luck or to forces outside our control rather than our own agency. Over time, this "forgetting" can lead to an unconscious downgrading of our capabilities. The capability journal is a practice for you: No one else is going to see what you write, so don't be shy about taking credit for the role you played in what went well that day. The practice doesn't need to take long, and the wins you recall can be simple, such as noting that you deftly turned down a project at work, that everyone in your family got ready on time that morning, that a difficult conversation went unexpectedly well, or that you felt especially connected to your partner over dinner. (The wins you celebrate can be big too, however!)

Expansion Move 3: Grab a Brag Buddy

Make a deal with a friend that every time you meet up for coffee or for a walk, each of you will spend the first five minutes bragging to one another about what is going well in your life. Set a timer so that each of you has an opportunity to speak. When it is your turn to brag, unabashedly celebrate what is going well for you. Exaggerate whatever joy, satisfaction, or happiness you may be experiencing. We recommend using gestures and sound as well, such as high fives, whoops, and the arms-up "touchdown" sign. Many of us have learned to outwardly downplay how good we might be feeling internally about something. When we do not allow our outward expression to match our internal experience, we deprive ourselves of fully experiencing just how good positive emotions feel.

While one person brags, the role of the other person is to listen and audibly celebrate alongside your brag buddy. Ask your partner what they did to create the successes they're celebrating. Many of us have had experiences in the past where we felt judged by others for our accomplishments. This practice is an opportunity to rewrite that history and to have lived experiences where we feel safe, connected, and close to others as we celebrate ourselves.

Expansion Move 4: Out Your Preferred Method of Deflecting Appreciation

There are usually underlying fears that stop us from receiving appreciation that are even deeper than not wanting to draw attention to ourselves or not wanting to make ourselves the target of other people's envy. For example, we might worry that we're creating an expectation that we will reciprocate. It can feel vulnerable to expose the fact that we care what other people think. We worry that we might be upping the bar for next time, and we don't know if we're up to delivering. Some of us are convinced that if we're told we're good at something, we'll become lazy and stop trying. And naturally, we worry that accepting appreciation means that we're not humble.

Because of these fears, most of us have developed strategies to deflect and minimize appreciation. Over time, these strategies can become so automatic that we're not even aware we're doing them. Here are some of the common strategies we use to deflect appreciation, which are adapted from the Conscious Leadership Group. As you read through the list, note which statements sound familiar to you and your preferred way to minimize appreciation. With new awareness of this habit, catch when you default to a deflection strategy when others are praising or recognizing you in real time. When you notice yourself deflecting, stop the thought, or even stop the statement midsentence, pause, and cultivate a new habit. Simply say, "Thank you." You will likely recognize all these maneuvers and favor a few in your own stories.

The Truth Denier: Deny the appreciation, including all supporting facts.
- "That can't possibly be true."
- "They're forgetting about . . ."

The Handoff: Pass or redirect the appreciation to someone else.
- "It wasn't really me."
- "It was a team effort."

The Impossible: Diminish the appreciation by comparing it to an ideal.
- "I could have done it better if I had . . ."
- "It was okay, but next time I will . . ."

The Skeptic: Question the motives of the appreciator.
- "They're only saying this because they want something from me."
- "They're trying to make me feel good about myself."

The Downgrade: Dismiss your actions as not worthy of note.
- "It was really no big deal."
- "Anyone could have done the same."

The Reciprocity Race: One-up with reciprocal appreciation.
- "It's so nice of you to see that."
- "I have seen you do the same."

Expansion Move 5: Build Your Capacity to Receive Appreciation

As you start to pay attention to how often you deflect and minimize the appreciation of others, you may notice uncomfortable sensations arising in your body as you shift to accepting rather than deflecting appreciation. These physical sensations of discomfort can cause us to shut down and shut out the upsides of appreciation: love, acknowledgment, acceptance, and a feeling of being seen. To expand your physical capacity to receive appreciation, we recommend that you take slow, deep breaths when you find yourself in situations where others are recognizing you. Notice what fears arise as you consciously breathe in compliments and notice whether any part of your body starts to contract or become rigid. If you find yourself becoming overwhelmed or you notice your body starting to shut down, ask others to slow down with their words of affirmation so that you can really take them in.

Expansion Move 6: Ask for Specific Feedback

Often, the recognition and acknowledgment that we receive can feel generic: "You did a great job." "You're really good at [insert activity]." If someone gives you a generic compliment, don't be afraid to ask for more specific feedback so that you can learn about your unique gifts and ways of being in the world. We often do not have an accurate map of our true capabilities, and the feedback of others is a useful tool to learn more about ourselves. Here are some specific questions you can ask others to help them elaborate on their recognition of you:

- "Would you provide me with one or two specific examples when you saw me really shining?"
- "When I was at my best, what did you notice me doing exactly?"
- "Thank you for this compliment. Did you notice a particular moment when I seemed especially alive or lit up during this activity/project?"
- "What do you notice that seems to come easily to me that is difficult for others?"
- "What is distinctive about the way I approach this activity in contrast to others?"

Expansion Move 7: Self-Source Approval

Many of us have a story that it is arrogant or egotistical to recognize our own talents or skills, and so we wait (or hope) that others will appreciate what we do. While acknowledgment from others is important, notice when you start to feel a sense of entitlement or expectation that others appreciate you. When you start to expect or feel entitled to appreciation, it is often a clue that there might be an unmet need for recognition, a need that is universal, yet one that you may have trouble naming, owning, and meeting on your own. Rather than outsourcing the meeting of your need for recognition, reframe rising sensations of entitlement and expectation as clues pointing to what you're wanting, and then meet that need yourself. Ask yourself what affirmation you'd like to hear from others and give it to yourself instead. Just as you would with any other praise or acknowledgment, breathe slowly and allow your words of self-acknowledgment to sink in.

4

GLUTTONY

Do you enjoy being in your body?

WHAT YOU'LL RECOVER: ACCESS TO FEELING COMFORTABLE IN YOUR SKIN AND EMBODYING PLEASURE

The story started with a woman and an apple—and it ended with eternal damnation. This is a story as old as stories, though we somehow haven't outgrown it. It still rings true for many women, who track every morsel they eat, every step they take, and every spike in their blood sugar on their continuous glucose monitors. We live in a world where health and vanity are inextricably linked, where we all subscribe to ideas of what a good body is: one that's compliant, conformist, and as small as possible. A good body is the obvious result of discipline and self-control. To live in a body that's otherwise—that's *bad,* or large—suggests deviance, or more specifically that you are an unruly person with no self-restraint, that you don't care, that you are unworthy of love and acceptance, that you are comfortable being a tax on the health care system, and so forth. Women can recite all of this in our sleep; it's been drummed into us since we saw our own mothers and grandmothers belittle themselves about their bodies. We also know the great doozy of a lie that weight is the result of a simple equation: Calories In = Calories Out.

While it seemed for a minute like we would all be able to relax within new frameworks of health at any size and body positivity, or at least neutrality, the pharmacological breakthroughs of Ozempic and Mounjaro are shifting the culture once again. You'll find the most prescriptions per capita on the Upper East Side of Manhattan, which last I checked was full of size 4s and not size 40s. Access to these appetite-suppressing drugs is making already thin wealthy women impossibly skinny, ensuring that our culture's current beauty standards remain impossibly out of reach.

As for those beauty standards, it's impossible to understand where they begin and where they end: We recognize that they've shifted over time and are highly dependent on the area of the world in which you live, and yet we continue to program our lives according to these arbitrary barometers.

When people ask me which chapter of *On Our Best Behavior* was easiest to write, the answer comes just as easily: the one on gluttony. I don't know any woman who does not live her life—and spend an inordinate amount of her energy—riding the seesaw between restricting and permitting. *I was bad last night; I'll be good today.* Or *I don't deserve this donut; I really shouldn't be eating this donut; if I had more self-control, I'd be putting this donut in the garbage disposal and not down my throat.*

Most of us treat our bodies like they're wild beasts that need to be brought to heel: We bridle them harshly and then tightly grip the reins, convinced that these bodies of ours will run away with us should we dare to let go. This is no way to live. It's constricted and tight, tedious and boring, and a waste of our vital energy—yet so many of us find ourselves continually caught up in this hostile relationship, unwilling to test the boundaries of what might happen if we let our bodies, and their appetites, lead. Or even live.

For some women, body size seems to be equated with health—there's a medical insistence that weight must be dropped and inches must be lost. Perhaps this is correct; perhaps this is fatphobic. But we also don't want to live in a world where we heap contempt on women who want something different for themselves—we can only hope that it's grounded in an internal longing and not compelled by social pressure or standards. Women don't need to attend to more imposed conflict: We are judged enough; we should be allowed to choose.

It's interesting to me that the apparent antidote—these GLP-1 inhibitors—severs the appetite and cuts it off at the root. The answer to our woes about food and weight seems to be to insist that we have no hunger at all, to eliminate it, to sap the pleasure right out of our days. After all, taste is one of the ways we contact and experience the world, core to our very humanity. There must be a better way to find mutual respect and balance between body and mind, to reestablish trust and ease and even love.

That's the goal of this section: to interrogate the stories we tell about how our bodies show up in the world and to stop interrogating our bodies directly—to come to a place of peace, an allowance of joy and pleasure, and a stance of gratitude for everything our bodies enable us to do and be.

Before we get to it, we wanted to make another note about appetite suppression: Many of us are emotional eaters, meaning that we center celebrations on shared meals, show love by baking a cake, or eat our feelings in front of Netflix when we've had a bad day. When appetite disappears and this soothing mechanism goes with it, people report feeling bereft at the absence of one of their primary tools for processing—or numbing—their days. This can create a lot of angst and anxiety. If you're in this boat, perhaps some of the tools we offer can replace the late-night snacks.

CORE PROCESS APPLIED TO THE SIN OF GLUTTONY
Tool 1: Is It a Fact or Is It a Story?
Excavating Unconscious Stories

For a full explanation of this tool, see page 10.

First, brainstorm some facts relevant to your relationship to appetite and the size of your body. We've offered some examples below.

FACTS ABOUT GLUTTONY

Elise Example: I've gained fifteen pounds in the last few years.

Courtney Example: I wear a size 8.

YOUR FACTS:

1. _____

2. _____

3. _____

Tip: Are these facts capable of being documented by a video recorder? For example, "I've gained fifteen pounds in the last few years" is a fact. "There's something wrong with how I look" is a story.

Second, brainstorm the stories that you make up about these facts.

STORIES I MAKE UP ABOUT GLUTTONY

Elise's Fact 1: I've gained fifteen pounds in the last few years.

Stories Elise makes up about that fact: If I lose this weight, I'll be prioritizing body image in a way that annoys me and feels in conflict with how I've also changed. I'm past this shit.

There's something wrong with how I look.

If I'm not really careful and hypervigilant about what I eat, I'll gain even more weight.

Courtney's Fact 1: I wear a size 8.

Stories Courtney makes up about that fact: I have to watch my weight really carefully in order to maintain this size.

I'm not overweight, but it would be great if I were smaller. A lot of my friends are thinner than I am.

I spend a lot of time and energy maintaining my weight.

Fact 1: _____

Stories you make up
about that fact: _____

_____

_____

Fact 2: _____

Stories you make up
about that fact: _____

_____

_____

Fact 3: _____

Stories you make up
about that fact: _____

_____

_____

Third, use the questions on the next page to help you brainstorm some of the additional stories you have about gluttony.

- What stories do you make up about your weight?
- What stories do you make up about your physical appearance?
- What stories do you make up about your body and its hunger?
- What stories do you make up about women who are overweight?
- What stories do you make up about women who are old?

Elise Examples:

- Women who care about the size of their bodies are wasting their time and energy—who cares? (I care.)
- Women who look good are rich in time and resources.
- You can't eat what you want and be "small."

Courtney Examples:

- As I age, I will become less attractive.
- I would gain a lot of weight if I started eating what my body wants.
- I'm too busy to exercise as much as I should.

YOUR STORIES:

1. _____

2. _____

3. _____

4. _____

5. _____

Now that you've excavated some of the stories that underlie your relationship to the size of your body and appetite, go back through what you've written and star the two or three that drive you the most. Those are the stories that we recommend working with throughout the rest of this chapter.

Tool 2: And Then What?

Tracing the Acting, Sensing, Feeling, and Thinking Loop

For a full description of this tool, see page 13.

Take the first story you want to work with from your starred list. You can repeat this process as many times as you want with different stories.

Story: _____

Step 1: What Actions Do You Take?

When I choose to believe this story, this is how I show up in the world:

My behaviors are: _____

I start to prioritize: _____

My attention goes to: _____

Three specific examples where I notice this story driving my behavior are:

When I: _____

When I: _____

When I: _____

Step 2: What Sensations Do You Feel?

When I choose to believe this story, I experience the following sensations in my body:

In my forehead, I feel:

Swirling	Fogginess	Buzziness
Spaciousness	Density	Sharpness
Scattered	Throbbing	Stirred up

In the back of my neck, across my shoulders, and in my jaw, I feel:

Tight	Twisted	Pulling
Bunched	Itchy	Burning
Cord-like	Clenched	Steely
Rigid	Blocky	Prickly

Across my high chest and upper throat, I feel:

Heaviness	Constriction	Cut off
Closed in	Numb	Melting
Compressed	Achy	Pierced
Unable to breathe	Flatness	Cold

Around the stomach area, I feel:

Knotted	Fluttering	Butterflies
Nauseous	Braced	Hollow
Churning	Empty	Doubled-over

In other parts of my body, I feel:

Racing heart	Trembling hands	Low-energy
Collapsed	Wiggly	Teary
Expanded	Tingly	Stretched

These tables are adapted from Gay and Katie Hendricks's work on body sensations and intelligence. See www.hendricks.com for further information.

Step 3: What Feelings Do You Have?

When I choose to believe this story, I experience the following emotions:

Anger

LOW	MEDIUM	HIGH
Annoyed	Agitated	Enraged
Bored	Disgusted	Furious
Bothered	Frustrated	Hostile
Dissatisfied	Indignant	Livid
Irritable	Irritated	Outraged
Tense	Resentful	Vengeful

Sadness

LOW	MEDIUM	HIGH
Blue	Discouraged	Agony
Down	Gloomy	Anguished
Lonely	Hopeless	Devastated
Somber	Melancholic	Heartbroken
Solemn	Regretful	Grief-stricken
Unhappy	Sorrowful	Mourning

Fear

LOW	MEDIUM	HIGH
Concerned	Apprehensive	Frightened
Guarded	Edgy	Frozen
Hesitant	Jumpy	Panicked
Reluctant	Nervous	Petrified
Suspicious	Startled	Shocked
Vulnerable	Worried	Terrified

Joy

LOW	MEDIUM	HIGH
Calm	Cheerful	Blissful
Carefree	Excited	Delighted
Content	Graceful	Ecstatic
Lighthearted	Optimistic	Enthusiastic
Peaceful	Proud	Elated
Relaxed	Thankful	Expansive

These tables are excerpted with permission from the Conscious Leadership Group's work on emotions. See www.conscious.is for further information.

Step 4: What Thoughts Come Next?

When I choose to believe this story, the following thoughts arise:

I begin to think that:_____

I judge myself as: _____

I judge others [insert name] as: _____

Tool 3: Why Stories Stick

Identifying the Underlying Fear

For a full description of this tool and the corresponding "Flavors of Fear" chart, see page 22.

Take one of the stories that you excavated in Tool 1 and explored in Tool 2. We're now going to investigate the fear activated by this particular story.

You can repeat this exercise for as many stories as you wish.

On page 144, we have included examples of this process using our own stories.

Story: _____

When I believe this story and consider the actions, body sensations, emotions, and thinking patterns that it generates, what flavor(s) of fear does it most directly map onto?

- Fight
- Flee
- Freeze
- Fawn
- Faint

Tip: If this exercise feels difficult for you, you might consider standing up, repeating your story aloud a few times, and exaggerating the posture your body takes on as you go into the story.

If I were to disregard this story, what am I afraid might happen?

_____

What am I *really* afraid might happen?

_____

Tip: You may need to ask the question "What am I *really* afraid might happen?" a few times in order to get at the root fear that is activated. There is no wrong answer here, just an intention to understand and be with your own experience a bit more.

Does that fear seem most related to:

- A loss of control?
- A loss of approval?
- A loss of security?

As you sit with what you've learned, see if you'd be willing to acknowledge and accept that there is a part of you that feels scared. The goal is to be with this fear rather than pushing it away.

EXAMPLES:

> Elise's Story: If I lose this weight, I'll be prioritizing body image in a way that annoys me and feels in conflict with how I've also changed. I'm past this shit.

Fear Flavor: Fight

If I were to disregard this story, what am I afraid might happen?

If I commit to losing this weight, people will think that I'm superficial and self-obsessed.

What am I *really* afraid might happen?

If I commit to losing this weight, people will think that I'm a sellout and promoting the cultural beauty standards that my work insists we abandon.

This fear is most related to: Approval

> Courtney's Story: I'm too busy to exercise as much as I should.

Fear Flavor: Fight and Faint

If I were to disregard this story, what am I afraid might happen?

I'd have to take responsibility for my body's health rather than blaming it on how hard I work or the demands of others.

What am I *really* afraid might happen?

I'd feel at peace with my body, and I wouldn't have anything to motivate me to take care of it.

This fear is most related to: Control

Tool 4: Welcome to the Drama Triangle
Relating to Stories from Victimhood Consciousness

Story: _____

For a comprehensive explanation of the Drama Triangle, see page 27.

Pick a specific situation in which this story shows up in your life (see the specific examples you listed in Tool 2 for the story you're working with).

Rotate through the three positions of the Drama Triangle and answer the following questions with respect to this situation/story.

You can write your answers down in this workbook and/or use this tool as an opportunity to stand up and voice your answers out loud. Either way, this is not the time to be polite. The Victim, Villain, and Hero all see reality through overly simplified and reductionist lenses. When you take on their voices, we encourage you to use raw and simple language. Write or speak plainly. No one else is reading this material. It's here for you and you alone. We even dare you to have fun.

THE VICTIM LENS

How are you hurt, taken advantage of, or burdened?

_____

What do you find yourself worrying about over and over again?

_____

Where do you feel overwhelmed, helpless, or ineffectual?

_____

In what ways do you feel that life is unfair?

_____

THE VILLAIN LENS

Who do you blame, hold responsible, or see as the enemy?

_____

What beliefs do you have 100 percent certainty about?

_____

What/who needs to do something different to fix this situation?

_____

What do you take very seriously?

_____

THE HERO LENS

How do you ensure you are needed?

_____

Where do you take on responsibilities that are not yours?

_____

What are you avoiding or suppressing?

_____

How do you minimize or distract yourself from any discomfort?

_____

REFLECTION

Which role in the Drama Triangle feels the most familiar to you?

_____

What are you most afraid of?

_____

What have you not yet fully faced or accepted about this situation?

_____

What truths or feelings have you not yet expressed about this situation?

_____

Tool 5: What Do These Stories Get You?

Owning the Payoffs and Costs of Our Unconscious Stories

Story: _____

Who taught me this story?

_____

What do I gain from believing this story?

_____

In what way does believing this story serve me?

_____

Who do I get to stay close with by believing this story?

_____

How do I keep this story going?

_____

If I didn't believe this story, what would I be doing instead?

_____

What does this story cost me?

_____

If I discard this story, what do I have to risk?

_____

How do I use this story to keep me from devoting my energy to that which makes me feel truly alive?

_____

In order to discard this story, what role, behavior, or way of being do I need to shed and grow out of?

_____

How would my relationship to myself change if I didn't believe this story?

_____

How would my relationship to [insert name] change if I didn't believe this story?

_____

These questions are adapted with permission from the Conscious Leadership Group's work on the Drama Triangle. See www.conscious.is for further information.

Tool 6: Teach the Class

Reclaiming Responsibility and Becoming the Creator

Story: _____

Remember: You're teaching this class at a women's college, and you want these twenty-somethings to buy into the exact same story that you are working with here. Your students need very specific instructions that they can follow to re-create and live by this story in their own lives. **The advice that you offer to your students should be actions, feelings, thoughts, and beliefs that they themselves can choose and have control over.** Really commit! Win that teaching prize!

Answer the questions that follow to help you create a game plan for your students:

What actions do you take or not take to ensure you keep believing this story?

_____

What other stories, beliefs, or thoughts should you have about yourself, others, or the world in order to keep this story going?

_____

What feelings should you repress or conceal so that this story remains the same?

_____

What do you withhold and from whom?

_____

What do you try to control that you actually can't?

_____

What do you need to believe you are right about?

_____

What agreements do you have to make and/or break with yourself or with others?

_____

What matters the most to you?

_____

What do you need to feel afraid of losing?

_____

What other "shoulds" do you need to believe?

_____

Now that you have reflected on the specific ways you have ensured that this particular story remains integral in your life, what are you willing to take responsibility for and do differently?

_____

The "Teach the Class" exercise is excerpted with permission from the Conscious Leadership Group's work on personal responsibility. See www.conscious.is for further information.

Tool 7: Playing with Personas

Inviting All Parts of You to the Table

For a full description of this tool, see page 40.

When you believe the stories you have about gluttony, what persona shows up and dictates your way of being in the world?

EXAMPLES:

Weight Watcher Winona: My mood hinges on my daily date with my scale. If I'm more than one pound above my goal weight, I don't eat or I eat very little that day.

Betty Binge Crocker: I exercise impeccable self-control until I walk past the break room. Once I eat one brownie, it's over: I need three or four, or the whole pan. Then I feel ill and full of self-hatred.

Jane Fonda Junior: I work out compulsively. I am scared of what might happen if I take a day off.

YOUR PERSONAS:

Name and description: _____

Name and description: _____

GET TO KNOW YOUR PERSONA

Once you have a name for the persona who shows up when you believe your stories about gluttony, answer the following questions:

In what situations does this persona tend to show up?

_____

What are some classic phrases this persona often says or thinks?

_____

What behaviors and actions are typical for this persona?

_____

Think of a specific situation when this persona recently showed up, and allow him/her to directly answer the following questions:

What is the most important thing to you?

_____

How do you make [insert your own name]'s life better?

_____

When did you first make your appearance?

_____

Who did you learn your style from?

_____

What are you most afraid of?

_____

What do you most want?

_____

These questions are excerpted with permission from _Centering and the Art of Intimacy Handbook,_ by Gay and Katie Hendricks. See www.hendricks.com for further information.

THE PAYOFFS AND COSTS OF THIS PERSONA

When I adopt this persona,

I don't have to feel:

_____

I get to be right and make _____ wrong.

I get to control:

_____

I get to avoid:

_____

I get to feel safe by:

_____

But **when I adopt this persona,**

I don't get to try out:

_____

I don't get to enjoy:

_____

I lose the opportunity to:

_____

I lose this aspect of my humanity:

_____

These questions are adapted with permission from *Centering and the Art of Intimacy Handbook*, by Gay and Katie Hendricks. See www.hendricks.com for further information.

Expansion Moves for the Sin of Gluttony

If you could wipe out the influences of your family, culture, and past and instead approach your relationship to your body, appetite, and pleasure with fresh eyes, how would you act? What would you do and what would you believe? These expansion moves are designed to help you hit refresh and explore with curiosity and openness what you actually want your relationship to embodied pleasure to be. For more on these expansion moves, see page 44.

Expansion Move 1: Persona Play as a Form of Shadow Integration

We can do a lot with persona play: It's a way to explore parts of ourselves that are underdeveloped, parts of ourselves that "we would never do," parts of ourselves that we admire and feel attracted to in others, and conversely, parts of ourselves that we judge and feel an aversion to when we see these parts in other people. For more context on playing with shadow personas, refer to the explanation at the end of the "Sloth" chapter, on page 58.

We've outlined one persona here—essentially a woman who loves food, who enjoys eating, who experiences extreme sensorial pleasure because she embodies a relationship with food that we have observed is scary for many women (ourselves included). We call her Nubile Nigella. If this doesn't resonate for you, identify a different persona and follow the same process. Here is Nubile Nigella in her own words:

In my kitchen, no spoon goes unlicked, and no finger avoids being sucked—my mouth is my primary organ and everything is *yummy*! I eat my meals with my hands whenever I can. I want to taste and eat the entire world. After all, food is meant to be savored and enjoyed! I eat slowly; every meal is an opportunity to experience pleasure. I'm not shy about expressing what I like on my plate. I often moan, close my eyes, and grab the table with ecstasy as I taste my food. Eating is *so* much more fun this way.

When we expand into shadow personas, we bring forward aspects of ourselves that we usually deny or forbid. We can then confront the fears and judgments that prevent us from letting these aspects of ourselves show up in our ordinary lives. When working with the "gluttonous" persona Nubile Nigella, we suggest the following:

- Select a particular meal you'd like to eat or prepare in the style of Nubile Nigella.
- Give the people around you a heads-up that you're exploring a character or part of yourself that feels new or foreign to you. Explain that it's just a fun experiment and you'd like some support. This game is actually the most fun when others agree to participate alongside you. Some of my most favorite evenings have been when a few girlfriends and I have agreed to channel Nubile Nigella throughout the meal.
- Take on the persona of Nubile Nigella and embody her fully. Exaggerate her. Sometimes using a prop, accent, or funny voice or noise can be helpful to shift you out of your normal space. If a particular quality we've attributed to Nubile Nigella does not resonate with you or if you'd like to change her name, feel free to make a few tweaks to the character until she feels like your own.

- As you spend time as Nubile Nigella, notice what body sensations, emotions, and thoughts come up for you. Ask others what they think of the persona. What you learn might surprise you. You may consider playing the character a few times to see if your internal response to her changes over time. You may also find that you grow to love and appreciate Nigella's value.

Expansion Move 2: End Your Complicity

Take personal responsibility for our cultural judgments of women and their bodies. We are just as much active creators in our culture as anyone else. Make a commitment with your friends to end the practice of talking negatively about your own body—and refuse to listen to them deprecate their own. You *can* gently explore your feelings about food and size but without castigating yourself. In addition, end the practice of gossiping about women and their bodies, and whether you think they have "good" ones or "bad" ones. (Elise here, but I've developed a not-kind habit of conjecturing about who is on a GLP-1 drug like Ozempic or Mounjaro—really, it's none of my business, but the way that it makes me feel about my body is something for me to work on.) If you catch yourself judging a woman—whether a celebrity, a stranger, or someone in your circle—for how they look, voice the judgment out loud and use it for your own learning purposes.

Expansion Move 3: Mindful Eating

James Gordon, MD, is the founder of the Center for Mind-Body Medicine in Washington, D.C., where the focus is on healing trauma. Gordon and his team travel across the globe, helping groups affected by horrible events—school shootings, natural disasters, war—metabolize their experiences, access their grief, and move often-stuck emotions out of their bodies. One of the tools in their toolkit is a process of mindful eating, which is a helpful practice for all of us, traumatized or not. Many of us not only tend to self-soothe through eating mindlessly in front of the TV at night but typically eat too fast during meals, swallowing as much air as food. The primary point of mindful eating, besides getting us all to slow down and savor our meals, is that food can be incredibly grounding and pleasurable—it offers an opportunity to really be present in the moment and in our bodies. It's not uncommon when doing this practice to realize that you don't actually enjoy the taste of whatever it is that you're inhaling—or conversely, that something as simple as a crunch of crisp apple or a bite of chocolate ice cream can be sublime.

Gordon coaches people through this process by recommending that you place a piece of fruit on a plate, alongside a piece of dark chocolate. You can read about this and other trauma-informed exercises in *Transforming Trauma*.

- Before you begin, do three minutes of what he calls "Soft Belly Breathing," which can be difficult for women who police ourselves about holding our stomachs in. In this move, you let it go, breathing deeply into your relaxed belly.
- Notice and release any thoughts as they come up. Don't get after yourself for thinking about something unrelated to the task at hand; simply bring your attention back to your soft belly.
- Then look at the fruit and the chocolate and sit with yourself as you process whatever comes up for you. Where are you drawn? Are there judgments and chastisements about what you *should* choose in your head? Just notice and be with yourself.
- Pick up whatever you feel drawn to. Hold it, feel the texture, smell it, study it closely. Note any more thoughts or feelings.
- Next, put the piece of chocolate or fruit into your mouth without chewing—play with it with your tongue and sense into it fully.
- Chew at a tenth of the pace with which you normally do, noticing everything that's happening in your mouth and your mind.
- Journal: Describe the entire experience and anything that came up for you during this process.

One of the main takeaways—beyond becoming even more present to all the programming and stories in our heads—is that we don't really taste our food. This amazing sensorial experience, an experience that's often deeply pleasurable, is passing us by, simply because we're not actually tasting what's on our forks. Gordon recommends doing this every day or every other day for a week or so—or until you're able to slow yourself down. See Expansion Move 4 for what to do next.

Expansion Move 4: What Do I Even Like?

Elise here. Our modern world is replete with food rules about the qualities of a "good" diet. Not only is it all overwhelming and ever-changing, it's rigid. And it's somewhat nonsensical, as we're all highly individual: What tastes good to one person—and pleases their body—might very well make someone else feel bloated, constipated, or ill. Some people thrive as vegans; others feel like death. Some people live their best lives eating meat almost exclusively; others can't touch it. I know a lot about many of these styles of eating because I spent a long time in the world of wellness—and still I can't tell you what I should eat. It's confounding— and I've reached a point where I refuse to cut a class of food (e.g., gluten) arbitrarily.

Most recently, I started working with a doctor of Sasang constitutional medicine, which is a Korean system of single-needle acupuncture. I'll spare you all the details, but the theory is that there are eight constitutions distributed among us: two that are meat heavy, two that are vegetarian, and four in between. The constitutions are determined by the strength of the major organs: Your constitutional plan focuses on strengthening the weaker organs in your system to bring balance overall. What's so interesting to me about this system is that it posits that we knew what our bodies liked long ago—and are so disconnected from this internal compass that we've lost the plot, choosing our diets according to culture-wide edicts and not what actually tastes and feels good to us.

As my doctor told me my constitution—determined through muscle testing, pulse checking, and asking me a lot of questions—I was startled. He described me to a T: no hot exercise, nauseating. No shellfish, pork, cucumbers, beans, or celery (all things I have a strong aversion to, save the occasional strip of bacon). There were a few things I would miss—wheat, mushrooms, strawberries—but he gave things back to me that I had arbitrarily cut from my diet years ago, like dairy, corn, and all potatoes. Then he told me that I must start eating with a lot more frequency. No problem.

We're just at the beginning of our work together, but the most exciting part is that he promises that I'll begin to intuit what my body wants again—by clearing out these cobwebs and beginning to listen carefully.

To that end, how many things are you eating because you think you should? What have you said goodbye to because you're subscribed to a rigid set of rules? Start tracking your eating—not to restrict, or calorie count, or obsess—but to legitimately note: *Do I even like this stuff? Does this give me any pleasure or joy? What do I actually want?*

To answer that question, I recommend a practice from energy healer and Celtic shaman Prune Harris, who teaches several methods of muscle testing for using your body's own intelligence to intuitively determine what your body wants: Does it want that glass of water? Does it want a Diet Coke? (Don't pre-judge your tests, as you might be surprised.) She explains the various processes more deeply on her website, "Self-Testing," and offers a YouTube video where you can watch her do this and learn how to do it on yourself. Do *not* do this with medicines; you can try it on supplements, though. The easiest way, in our experience, is to sit up with your feet flat on the ground. Place your right palm on your right knee and lift up with your leg firmly pressing into your palm, so you can feel strong pressure. Do this a few times. Then take the object in question—a bottle of juice, a bag of chips, an apple—and hold it near your solar plexus, immediately below the heart in the center line of your body. You're effectively bringing this object into your energy. Place your right palm on your knee while you do this and press up—Is it equally strong or much weaker? If the former, your body would be psyched for whatever is in your left hand. If it's weaker, it doesn't like it. If you want to test more items, rub your leg vigorously and then test again, first pressing up before you try it with an item. Here are some more tips from Prune—and remember, if this process doesn't work, she offers several others on her site (pruneharris.com).

- Practice self-testing with easy yes/no truths, like "My name is Elise." After you test your real name, try someone else's: "My name is Madonna" or "My name is Homer Simpson."
- Don't worry if you're not 100 percent accurate—as you practice, your accuracy will increase.
- Make sure you're well-hydrated.
- If you're feeling ungrounded, scattered, or stressed, Prune recommends

rubbing your feet with a spoon to correct the polarity in your body. Make sure the spoon is magnetic—you can use a fridge magnet to test. I like this process because even if it sounds like hocus-pocus, you're still bringing your body into the equation and pausing to ask it a question about what it wants. Nothing bad can come from this.

Expansion Move 5: Eating as an Expression of Deeper Needs

For many of us, our relationship with food points to our relationship with our broader need to nourish, soothe, and comfort ourselves. While we recognize and provide for these needs in children, we often give short shrift to them in adults. Many of us turn to food as a convenient source of comfort both because we lack awareness of what we really need and because we do not value ourselves sufficiently to believe these needs are worth meeting. Every time we reach for food when we're not hungry or, alternatively, every time we impose an external rule about what or how much we're "allowed" to eat, rather than listening to our bodies, we are cutting ourselves off from our bodies' intuitive understanding of what we need to regulate and sustain ourselves, what we need in order to thrive.

Rather than examining our relationship with food from a place of judgment, working with the "sin" of gluttony from a place of curiosity invites us into conscious awareness and relationship with our deeper need for fundamental self-care. The exploration of our deeper needs starts with asking the question "What body sensations, feelings, and thoughts arise within me when I explicitly acknowledge my need for nourishment, soothing, and comfort?" Close your eyes and say out loud, "I have a need to nourish and take care of myself. I have a need to soothe myself. I have a need to comfort myself." Notice the sensations, feelings, and stories that arise when you consciously claim these needs, and use the core process as necessary.

Next, ask yourself, "What are the body sensations that tell me I need nourishing? What are the body sensations that tell me I need soothing or comfort?" We recommend you write your answers down or even draw a picture of how these needs manifest in your body.

Next, ask yourself, "How do I know that something is meeting these needs?

What are the signals and sensations in my body that tell me that an activity is nourishing, soothing, or comforting? Are the signals and sensations of soothing or comfort different from actual self-care?" Again, we invite you to write your answers down or draw a picture. The objective of both practices is to cultivate awareness of how your body signals what it needs and whether these needs are being met.

Last, we invite you to make a list of the activities you find nourishing, self-loving, soothing, or comforting. How often do you practice these activities? Which would you like to practice more or less of? We recommend that you post your list in a few prominent locations so that you remember and expand your toolkit for nourishing, soothing, and caring for yourself.

Expansion Move 6: Mirror Work

Take some time to look at your body naked in the mirror. You might start with noticing your overall impression of your body: Do you like it? What judgments—positive or negative—arise? Then we recommend that you begin systematically focusing your attention on each part of your body. Start with your neck and work your way down to each body part: your collarbones, your shoulders, your upper arms, your forearms, your wrists, your hands, your upper chest, your breasts, your upper abdomen, your lower abdomen, your upper and lower back (if you can see them), your hips, your pubic area, your vulva, your upper thighs, your behind (if you can see it), your knees, your calves, your ankles, and your feet.

See if you can imagine that each body part does not belong to you and that you're looking at them on another person. Narrate to yourself what each of these body parts looks like. Notice the shape of each body part, its size, and the color and texture of your skin. Notice whether you're using factual or value-based statements to describe the various parts. If you notice judgment arising about any body part, whether positive or negative, ask yourself whether you would have this judgment if you had never seen this body part before. For example, if you've never seen a knee before, how do you know which knees are beautiful and which are not?

We recommend giving yourself ample time for this exercise. When it's finished, has your relationship to your body changed or stayed the same?

Expansion Move 7: Write a Thank-You Note to Your Body

Write a letter to your body acknowledging and thanking it for all it has done. Address your letter: Dear Body, and sign your letter: Love, [insert your name]. Some questions to consider as you write your note of thanks:

- What injuries, illnesses, or even miracles has your body sustained and survived?
- What activities has your body learned to do?
- What activities has your body accomplished?
- What activities does your body do every day without you thinking about it?
- What does your body know?
- What and how does your body communicate?
- How does your body protect you?
- What pleasures have you experienced because you have a body?

When you have finished writing your letter, read it aloud.

5

❧

GREED

Do you feel like you have enough?

WHAT YOU'LL RECOVER: ACCESS TO FEELINGS OF SAFETY AND SECURITY AND AN ESCAPE FROM A SCARCITY MINDSET

You likely know the adage: Don't talk about politics, sex, or money in "polite" company—historically, "polite" being the exclusive domain of women. Men, in the company of other men, have never been so restricted; this is perhaps just one of the reasons that the worlds of finance and government have proven so exclusionary to women. Money, we're told, is not for us. And in many ways, this has been true: It wasn't until the Equal Credit Opportunity Act passed in 1974 that a woman could get a credit card in her own name. (Interestingly, the Equal Pay Act passed a decade earlier, in 1963—though eighty years later, we've yet to see our compensation balance out.)

We know the related stories: Women are bad with money because of those pesky latte habits. We really should learn how to budget. It's also our patriotic duty to spend money to support the economy—particularly during times of threat or crisis, when we should care more about the survival of corporations than our own savings account. This is how the wider culture speaks to women about money. As Kara Loewentheil reports in her 2024 book *Take Back Your Brain,* "A 2018 study from Starling Bank looked at three hundred finance articles from various countries and found that 65 percent of the articles aimed at women characterized them as 'splurgers.' Nearly 90 percent of female-targeted financial articles advised women to 'cut back' on their spending." You know the drill: We're bad with money, while men are inherently and intuitively skilled.

This is funny, though, because women have been proven to be better investors, which researchers attribute to our willingness to do more research, our trading *less,* and our having less testosterone to fuel feelings of overconfidence. We're also far more generous and charitable (shout-out to MacKenzie Scott and Melinda Gates), underlying one of my key presuppositions: The world would be far better off if women had more money. I use this idea to work on my own discomfort and deep ambivalence about making more money.

Like most of us, I've been conditioned to believe that money is base—and that wanting more of it is immoral. This discomfort is borne out by the wealth inequalities that continue to rage across the world. It doesn't feel good to be one of the haves when there are so many have-nots, particularly for women, who tend to care deeply about the suffering and well-being of others. Our current state of capitalism can also be a hard pill to swallow when we look at the earth's inability to keep pace with our rampant consumerism. The math just doesn't add up. Many women I know have absolutely no interest in making our collective problems worse.

According to Lynne Twist, the author of *The Soul of Money,* women see money as bounded, limited, and scarce, like a pond, while men are more inclined to experience money as an ever-abundant river of 0s and 1s. The psychology of this is: *If I get more, you get less.* Meanwhile, for men, the vibe is different: *There's more where this came from, and my take makes no discernible impact on the whole.* Meanwhile, although it is tethered to the gold standard, which is a finite, highly valuable, scarce material good, money really is a form of energy, particularly in our digital world where we rarely even touch currency.

This belief that we're taking from a limited pie and that our advantages might directly distress someone else certainly haunts the minds of women. This might be the one valid reason that women are accused of being poor negotiators (and, therefore, maddeningly blamed for perpetuating the pay gap). But it's really only half the story. In reality, women are excellent negotiators—in many instances, far better at advocating on behalf of other people's needs, sitting in silence, and reading the energy and emotion of a room than men. Where we struggle is in advocating and negotiating on behalf of our own interests (cue: selfishness!)—in part because we're judged harshly by both men and women when we act outside of the cultural codes of femininity. Women are policed when we're perceived as being ambitious, assertive, or aggressive.

While we talk a lot about the pay gap, we don't talk enough about the gender wealth gap: According to Ellevest's Sallie Krawcheck, for every dollar a white man owns, a white woman owns just 32 cents; for Black and Latina women, that amount drops to one penny. Yes, you read that right. This puts women and families in perilous positions: While it's impossible to engineer certainty in our world, to ensure our safety and security, access to money is one of the only factors that gives you any control over your environment. Girls, women—and, by extension, their families—need to have enough.

The idea of "enough" is very difficult to define—and it will likely be the subject of many of your stories in the following pages. Many of us subscribe to if/then statements: If I get into that college, then I'm assured a stable career. If I get that promotion, then I'll be able to get a new house. If I land that extra client, then I'll never have to worry about money again. This is the hamster wheel on which so many of us run. But while our culture would insist that money is the primary value and the solution to all of our woes should we manage to get more of it, *money does not solve emotional problems.* It can certainly make life a lot easier and solve a lot of concerns that drive anxiety, but more money will not cure all of our emotional wounds. The work remains.

One of the healers I work with routinely is a woman named Anne Emerson. On a recent call, she explained that she doesn't like the word *manifestation* because of the cultural baggage it has picked up in recent decades. "I think of manifestation as losing the internal conflict," she explained. For me, this felt like a huge unlock, specifically around my own deep ambivalence. As she pointed out, for someone who claims to not care about money, I've organized my entire life around making more of it. "You don't care about status," she explained. "But you care about money, and that's okay." I'm guessing that many of you can relate: I value money not for what it can provide, not because I think it will solve my deeper issues, but for the relative freedom it can grant. Let's find your money stories too.

CORE PROCESS APPLIED TO THE SIN OF GREED
Tool 1: Is It a Fact or Is It a Story?
Excavating Unconscious Stories

For a full explanation of this tool, see page 10.

First, brainstorm some facts relevant to your relationship to money, scarcity, and feelings of enough-ness. We've offered some examples below.

FACTS ABOUT GREED

Elise Example: I'm the primary breadwinner.

Courtney Example: My husband is the primary breadwinner.

YOUR FACTS:

1. _____

2. _____

3. _____

Tip: Are these facts capable of being documented by a video recorder? For example, "I'm the primary breadwinner" is a fact. "My husband doesn't make enough money" is a story.

Second, brainstorm the stories that you make up about these facts.

STORIES I MAKE UP ABOUT GREED

Elise's Fact 1:	I'm the primary breadwinner.
Stories Elise makes up about that fact:	All the pressure is on me; if my projects don't succeed or people stop hiring me, we'll be homeless soon.

My husband only married me and stays with me because I'm such a good worker.

My primary value to my kids is paying for things.

Courtney's Fact 1: My husband is the primary breadwinner.

Stories Courtney makes up about that fact: I should volunteer or not charge market value for my work since my husband makes enough money.

My husband's time is more valuable than mine since he makes more money than I do.

I need to run all financial decisions by my husband.

Fact 1: _____

Stories you make up about that fact: _____

_____

_____

Fact 2: _____

Stories you make up about that fact: _____

_____

_____

Fact 3: _____

Stories you make up
about that fact: _____

_____

_____

Third, use the questions below to help you brainstorm some of the additional stories you have about greed.

- What stories do you make up about your net worth?
- What stories do you make up about your ability to retire?
- What stories do you make up about your annual income?
- What stories do you make up about talking about money?
- What stories do you make up about women who are rich?
- What stories do you make up about women who are poor?

Elise Examples:

- If I accept money from someone, then they own me.
- I have a lot of judgment toward wealthy women and wonder if they really deserve their wealth or whether they're giving enough money away. On one hand, I feel like I give away as much as I can; on the other, I know I can always give away more.
- I'll never make enough money; it's impossible.

Courtney Examples:

- It's uncouth and shallow to speak frankly about how much money you make or want.
- Others might find me greedy if I dare to raise my prices.
- No one's financial status is as stable as they think. Forces beyond our control—a global pandemic or a recession—can eat up and destroy our savings in the blink of an eye.

YOUR STORIES:

1. _____

2. _____

3. _____

4. _____

5. _____

Now that you've excavated some of the stories that underlie your relationship to money, go back through what you've written and star the two or three that drive you the most. Those are the stories that we recommend working with throughout the rest of this chapter.

Tool 2: And Then What?

Tracing the Acting, Sensing, Feeling, and Thinking Loop

For a full description of this tool, see page 13.

Take the first story you want to work with from your starred list. You can repeat this process as many times as you want with different stories.

Story: _____

Step 1: What Actions Do You Take?

When I choose to believe this story, this is how I show up in the world:

My behaviors are: _____

I start to prioritize: _____

My attention goes to: _____

Three specific examples where I notice this story driving my behavior are:

When I: _____

_____

When I: _____

_____

When I: _____

Step 2: What Sensations Do You Feel?

When I choose to believe this story, I experience the following sensations in my body:

In my forehead, I feel:

Swirling	Fogginess	Buzziness
Spaciousness	Density	Sharpness
Scattered	Throbbing	Stirred up

In the back of my neck, across my shoulders, and in my jaw, I feel:

Tight	Twisted	Pulling
Bunched	Itchy	Burning
Cord-like	Clenched	Steely
Rigid	Blocky	Prickly

Across my high chest and upper throat, I feel:

Heaviness	Constriction	Cut off
Closed in	Numb	Melting
Compressed	Achy	Pierced
Unable to breathe	Flatness	Cold

Around the stomach area, I feel:

Knotted	Fluttering	Butterflies
Nauseous	Braced	Hollow
Churning	Empty	Doubled-over

In other parts of my body, I feel:

Racing heart	Trembling hands	Low-energy
Collapsed	Wiggly	Teary
Expanded	Tingly	Stretched

These tables are adapted from Gay and Katie Hendricks's work on body sensations and intelligence. See www.hendricks.com for further information.

Step 3: What Feelings Do You Have?

When I choose to believe this story, I experience the following emotions:

Anger

LOW	MEDIUM	HIGH
Annoyed	Agitated	Enraged
Bored	Disgusted	Furious
Bothered	Frustrated	Hostile
Dissatisfied	Indignant	Livid
Irritable	Irritated	Outraged
Tense	Resentful	Vengeful

Sadness

LOW	MEDIUM	HIGH
Blue	Discouraged	Agony
Down	Gloomy	Anguished
Lonely	Hopeless	Devastated
Somber	Melancholic	Heartbroken
Solemn	Regretful	Grief-stricken
Unhappy	Sorrowful	Mourning

Fear

LOW	MEDIUM	HIGH
Concerned	Apprehensive	Frightened
Guarded	Edgy	Frozen
Hesitant	Jumpy	Panicked
Reluctant	Nervous	Petrified
Suspicious	Startled	Shocked
Vulnerable	Worried	Terrified

Joy

LOW	MEDIUM	HIGH
Calm	Cheerful	Blissful
Carefree	Excited	Delighted
Content	Graceful	Ecstatic
Lighthearted	Optimistic	Enthusiastic
Peaceful	Proud	Elated
Relaxed	Thankful	Expansive

These tables are excerpted with permission from the Conscious Leadership Group's work on emotions. See www.conscious.is for further information.

Step 4: What Thoughts Come Next?

When I choose to believe this story, the following thoughts arise:

I begin to think that: _____

I judge myself as: _____

I judge others [insert name] as: _____

Tool 3: Why Stories Stick

Identifying the Underlying Fear

For a full description of this tool and the corresponding "Flavors of Fear" chart, see page 22.

Take one of the stories that you excavated in Tool 1 and explored in Tool 2. We're now going to investigate the fear activated by this particular story.

You can repeat this exercise for as many stories as you wish.

On pages 175 to 176, we have included examples of this process using our own stories.

Story: _____

When I believe this story and consider the actions, body sensations, emotions, and thinking patterns that it generates, what flavor(s) of fear does it most directly map onto?

- Fight
- Flee
- Freeze
- Fawn
- Faint

Tip: If this exercise feels difficult for you, you might consider standing up, repeating your story aloud a few times, and exaggerating the posture your body takes on as you go into the story.

If I were to disregard this story, what am I afraid might happen?

_____

What am I *really* afraid might happen?

_____

Tip: You may need to ask the question "What am I *really* afraid might happen?" a few times in order to get at the root fear that is activated. There is no wrong answer here, just an intention to understand and be with your own experience a bit more.

Does that fear seem most related to:

- A loss of control?
- A loss of approval?
- A loss of security?

As you sit with what you've learned, see if you'd be willing to acknowledge and accept that there is a part of you that feels scared. The goal is to be with this fear rather than pushing it away.

EXAMPLES:

Elise's Story: If I accept money from someone,
then they own me.

Fear Flavor: Freeze

If I were to disregard this story, what am I afraid might happen?

People will stop hiring me or wanting to work with me—a big part of my value is my immediate responsiveness and drop-everything attitude. I pride myself on overdelivering.

What am I _really_ afraid might happen?

Word will get out that I "underdeliver" or that I'm difficult. I'll lose everything.

This fear is most related to: Security

Courtney's Story: My husband's time is more valuable
than mine since he makes more money than I do.

Fear Flavor: Freeze and Fawn

If I were to disregard this story, what am I afraid might happen?

I'm afraid my husband and I would have more arguments and conflict about who does what around the house.

What am I *really* afraid might happen?

I'm afraid I won't know what value I add and contribute to our family and household.

This fear is most related to: Approval

Tool 4: Welcome to the Drama Triangle
Relating to Stories from Victimhood Consciousness

Story: _____

For a comprehensive explanation of the Drama Triangle, see page 27.

Pick a specific situation in which this story shows up in your life (see the specific examples you listed in Tool 2 for the story you're working with).

Rotate through the three positions of the Drama Triangle and answer the following questions with respect to this situation/story.

You can write your answers down in this workbook and/or use this tool as an opportunity to stand up and voice your answers out loud. Either way, this is not the time to be polite. The Victim, Villain, and Hero all see reality through overly simplified and reductionist lenses. When you take on their voices, we encourage you to use raw and simple language. Write or speak plainly. No one else is reading this material. It's here for you and you alone. We even dare you to have fun.

THE VICTIM LENS

How are you hurt, taken advantage of, or burdened?

_____

What do you find yourself worrying about over and over again?

_____

Where do you feel overwhelmed, helpless, or ineffectual?

_____

In what ways do you feel that life is unfair?

_____

THE VILLAIN LENS

Who do you blame, hold responsible, or see as the enemy?

_____

What beliefs do you have 100 percent certainty about?

_____

What/who needs to do something different to fix this situation?

_____

What do you take very seriously?

_____

THE HERO LENS

How do you ensure you are needed?

_____

Where do you take on responsibilities that are not yours?

_____

What are you avoiding or suppressing?

_____

How do you minimize or distract yourself from any discomfort?

_____

REFLECTION

Which role in the Drama Triangle feels the most familiar to you?

_____

What are you most afraid of?

_____

What have you not yet fully faced or accepted about this situation?

_____

What truths or feelings have you not yet expressed about this situation?

_____

Tool 5: What Do These Stories Get You?

Owning the Payoffs and Costs of Our Unconscious Stories

Story: _____

Who taught me this story?

_____

What do I gain from believing this story?

_____

In what way does believing this story serve me?

_____

Who do I get to stay close with by believing this story?

_____

How do I keep this story going?

_____

If I didn't believe this story, what would I be doing instead?

_____

What does this story cost me?

_____

If I discard this story, what do I have to risk?

_____

How do I use this story to keep me from devoting my energy to that which makes me feel truly alive?

_____

In order to discard this story, what role, behavior, or way of being do I need to shed and grow out of?

_____

How would my relationship to myself change if I didn't believe this story?

_____

How would my relationship to [insert name] change if I didn't believe this story?

_____

These questions are adapted with permission from the Conscious Leadership Group's work on the Drama Triangle. See www.conscious.is for further information.

Tool 6: Teach the Class

Reclaiming Responsibility and Becoming the Creator

Story: _____

Remember: You're teaching this class at a women's college, and you want these twenty-somethings to buy into the exact same story that you are working with here. Your students need very specific instructions that they can follow to re-create and live by this story in their own lives. **The advice that you offer to your students should be actions, feelings, thoughts, and beliefs that they themselves can choose and have control over.** Really commit! Win that teaching prize!

Answer the questions that follow to help you create a game plan for your students:

What actions do you take or not take to ensure you keep believing this story?

_____

What other stories, beliefs, or thoughts should you have about yourself, others, or the world in order to keep this story going?

_____

What feelings should you repress or conceal so that this story remains the same?

_____

What do you withhold and from whom?

_____

What do you try to control that you actually can't?

_____

What do you need to believe you are right about?

_____

What agreements do you have to make and/or break with yourself or with others?

_____

What matters the most to you?

_____

What do you need to feel afraid of losing?

_____

What other "shoulds" do you need to believe?

_____

Now that you have reflected on the specific ways you have ensured that this particular story remains integral in your life, what are you willing to take responsibility for and do differently?

_____

The "Teach the Class" exercise is excerpted with permission from the Conscious Leadership Group's work on personal responsibility. See www.conscious.is for further information.

Tool 7: Playing with Personas

Inviting All Parts of You to the Table

For a full description of this tool, see page 40.

When you believe the stories you have about greed, what persona shows up and dictates your way of being in the world?

EXAMPLES:

Bag Lady Bethie: No matter the amount I have in the bank, I'm scared it could vanish in an instant and I could wind up destitute.

Value Schmalue Valerie: I don't like talking about money, so I don't ask for raises, make counteroffers, or talk about what I make. I wouldn't want to be seen as greedy.

Polite Company Pattie: I'm uncomfortable talking about money. I don't have a long-term plan for money or financial security, and/or I delegate most financial decisions to my partner.

YOUR PERSONAS:

Name and description: _____

Name and description: _____

GET TO KNOW YOUR PERSONA

Once you have a name for the persona who shows up when you believe your stories about greed, answer the following questions:

In what situations does this persona tend to show up?

_____

What are some classic phrases this persona often says or thinks?

_____

What behaviors and actions are typical for this persona?

_____

Think of a specific situation when this persona recently showed up, and allow him/her to directly answer the following questions:

What is the most important thing to you?

_____

How do you make [insert your own name]'s life better?

_____

When did you first make your appearance?

_____

Who did you learn your style from?

_____

What are you most afraid of?

_____

What do you most want?

_____

These questions are excerpted with permission from _Centering and the Art of Intimacy Handbook,_ by Gay and Katie Hendricks. See www.hendricks.com for further information.

THE PAYOFFS AND COSTS OF THIS PERSONA

When I adopt this persona,

I don't have to feel:

_____

I get to be right and make _____ wrong.

I get to control:

_____

I get to avoid:

_____

I get to feel safe by:

_____

But **when I adopt this persona,**

I don't get to try out:

_____

I don't get to enjoy:

_____

I lose the opportunity to:

_____

I lose this aspect of my humanity:

_____

These questions are adapted with permission from *Centering and the Art of Intimacy Handbook,* by Gay and Katie Hendricks. See www.hendricks.com for further information.

Expansion Moves for the Sin of Greed

If you could wipe out the influences of your family, culture, and past and instead approach your relationship to money and scarcity with fresh eyes, how would you act? What would you do and what would you believe? These expansion moves are designed to help you hit refresh and explore with curiosity and openness what you want your relationship to feelings of "enough" to be. For more on these expansion moves, see page 44.

Expansion Move 1: Examine the Context in Which You Relate to Money

As Lynne Twist writes in *The Soul of Money,* the primary orientation of our culture to money is one of scarcity—*particularly* for women. The notion of scarcity is rooted in fear, fear arising from a belief that resources are inherently limited and must be competed for. While we've asked you to write down some of your core beliefs about money, it's worth additionally exploring what Lynne Twist calls "the three fundamental myths about money" that subtly and powerfully perpetuate our culture's scarcity orientation.

The three myths are:

- There is not enough, meaning that the resource of money is inherently limited and that I must organize my life around ensuring I get enough for myself and for those I care for. My ability to secure money comes at the expense of your ability to secure money.
- More is better, meaning that, because the resource of money is limited, it is better for me to accumulate as much as I can to ensure I always have enough. Because more is better, those who have more money are, by definition, better than those who have less.
- There is nothing I can do, meaning that the process by which money accrues to some people and not to others has certain unchangeable characteristics, limiting the terms and conditions through which money can be exchanged or accumulated.

In this exercise, we'd like you to reflect on your relationship to these three myths, examining where they might be true and alive within you.

Myth 1: Where in my life do I operate from the belief that "There is not enough"?

_____

_____

_____

_____

Myth 2: Where in my life do I operate from the belief that "More is better"?

_____

_____

_____

_____

Myth 3: Where in my life do I operate from the belief that "There is nothing I can do"?

We also suggest that you return to the core process and repeat the Tool 2, "And Then What?," for each of these three myths. (*Myth* is another word for story, after all, and these three beliefs might be the most powerful and foundational stories about money that we have.)

Expansion Move 2: Replace Scarcity with Sufficiency

The three fundamental myths of money contribute to a broader, foundational belief system: the mindset of scarcity. While many have defined the opposite of the scarcity mindset to be one of abundance, Twist asks us to instead cultivate a mindset of sufficiency. Cultivating a sufficiency mindset does not mean disregarding, ignoring, or going passive about our relationship to money and other resources. Rather, it's about consciously choosing the context or larger frame of reference in which we relate to money—its earning, saving, investment, accumulation, allocation, and distribution. When you relate to money, not from a place of scarcity or fear, but from a place of sufficiency or enoughness, how does your experience shift? How do you feel in your body and heart? How do you act? How do you treat others? How do you treat yourself? How do you spend your time? What thoughts arise?

It is tempting to believe that the facts of our financial circumstances determine whether we relate to money from a frame of scarcity or sufficiency. That said, in our experience, as well as what research and countless anecdotal stories in the press recount, it's more accurate to say that the two exist independently from each other—there are people who objectively have "plenty" of money who still relate from the place of scarcity. The context in which we choose to relate to money—

one of scarcity or one of sufficiency—is ultimately up to us. We want you to imagine what it might feel like to orient to money with a mindset of sufficiency rather than one of scarcity.

If I were to believe that there is enough money in this world, that more is not necessarily better, and that I am the ultimate creator of my relationship to money:

What sensations would arise in my body? (Close your eyes and tune inward for a moment before answering.)

_____

What emotions would I feel?

_____

What new and different thoughts would arise for me?

_____

How would I treat myself and others differently?

_____

How would I act and spend my time differently?

_____

Expansion Move 3: Expand Your Definition of Richness

One consequence of the pervasiveness of the scarcity mindset in our culture with respect to money is that it devalues the many, many other resources we possess. This is one of the ways that an attitude of scarcity around money becomes self-fulfilling. When we selectively focus on money as the sole resource through which we believe we can achieve freedom, security, peace, and so on, we overlook other resources at our disposal that just as powerfully shape our lives. We experience ourselves as lacking because we forget how broadly resourced we already are. One other consequence of the scarcity mindset is that it stops us from creating our own internal system as to what values, experiences, and talents matter to us. Money becomes the ultimate arbiter of value.

Courtney here. My good friend and colleague Holly Grant is a pioneer in the field of consciousness and money, and she has brainstormed a list of more than a hundred other resources/currencies that we forget about when we buy into the stories we've inherited about money and its power. We'd like you to conduct a similar practice here.

In addition to money, what other resources do I have access to? (Don't rush this question; take some time to ruminate and see what arises.) To get you started, here is a quick list I brainstormed.

Courtney's Examples:

- Access to a beautiful landscape and nature
- Strong friendships and community with women who live nearby
- Physical health, high energy, and stamina
- A curious mind that seeks out rigor, precision, and novelty
- The capacity to feel big emotions
- Skills around candor and broaching difficult conversations
- Family living nearby and close relationships with said family
- A self-commitment to growth and change
- Supportive mentors, friends, and clients who champion my work
- Schools that meet the academic and emotional needs of my children
- An extended network of family and friends who love and see my children as much as I do
- A huge library at home and one within walking distance
- The ability to be outside and in the sunshine most of the day, year-round
- A big sense of humor, laugh, and capacity for playfulness
- Better than average dance moves
- Work that feels like a calling

Once you've written up your list, it is useful to assign a monetary value to each resource. Ask, "How much money would someone have to pay me to give up [insert resource]?" You may find this illuminating and helpful to guide you toward your own, internal valuing of resources.

Expansion Move 4: See Money as a Neutral Instrument

Money is a currency, not a resource. What we mean by that is that money has no inherent value on its own. It is a means through which we accumulate other things that we value: shelter, food, education, possessions, experiences, et cetera. But because money has become the dominant and most explicit currency through which we purchase items of value, it has taken on an outsized role in our society and is seen as valuable for its own sake.

When we relate to money as an inherently valuable resource rather than as a value-neutral instrument or currency, we begin to go unconscious as to what we expect money to do for us. We begin to view money as a problem-solver of all kinds, without examining whether money buys what we're actually looking for.

Many of us are convinced that money or other possessions are the solution to our broader, nonmaterial needs as well as our emotional problems, that if we finally get the job, the house, or the vacation, we'll be—to quote psychiatrist Phil Stutz—"exonerated from pain, uncertainty, and the need for constant work." Money *can* solve a lot of practical problems—we need food, housing, health care—but over a certain amount (about $95,000 a year is an ideal annual income in the United States for individuals—families with children need more), more money does not contribute to more happiness. In fact, it can create more problems: People's lives often expand to fit their budgets (Bigger house! Nicer car!), meaning they never outrun their original anxiety. As we discussed in Expansion Move 2, the mindset of scarcity exists independent of our material wealth.

The goal of this exercise is to explore what you're expecting money and acquisitions to do for you. By using "If I just" statements, explore whether "enough" money will solve problems. Courtney has given an example to demonstrate how this exercise works.

Courtney's Example:
If I just had enough money, then I could stop thinking about money.

Then answer the following:

Is the above statement really true?

> As I imagine having enough money, it's actually not true that I would stop thinking about it. There would still be bills to pay and savings/investments/gifts/donations to consider. The more I think about what I wrote, the more it seems to me that, the more money I have, the *more* I might end up thinking about it.

What does the statement after "then" suggest that I really want?

> I could stop thinking about money. What do I really want when I say I want to stop thinking about money? I guess what I'm wanting is to stop worrying about money and to feel a greater sense of peace.

Does the statement after "If I just" actually get me what I really want?

> If I'm really honest, I can see that worrying about money and feeling a greater sense of peace are under my control and have very little to do with how much money I have. I can see that I actually have plenty of money and that I'm the one choosing to relate to it with anxiety.

YOUR EXAMPLES:

If I just _____ **, then** _____ .

Is the above statement really true?

_____

_____

What does the statement after "then" suggest that I really want?

_____

_____

Does the statement after "If I just" actually get me what I really want?

_____

_____

If I just _____, **then** _____.

Is the above statement really true?

_____

_____

What does the statement after "then" suggest that I really want?

_____

_____

Does the statement after "If I just" actually get me what I really want?

_____

_____

If I just _____, **then** _____.

Is the above statement really true?

_____

_____

What does the statement after "then" suggest that I really want?

_____

_____

Does the statement after "If I just" actually get me what I really want?

_____

_____

Expansion Move 5: Uncover Your Deeper Values and Needs

When we relate to money with a scarcity mindset, not only do we obscure and devalue our access to broader resources, but we also obscure and lose contact with our deeper needs and desires. The therapist and writer Francis Weller makes the distinction between sources of primary satisfaction and secondary satisfaction. Primary satisfactions hearken back to basic ways human beings have taken care of themselves for thousands of years. They include things like communal eating, making music and art, dancing, time in nature, touch and affection, collecting and preparing food, sacred ritual, contemplation, and ceremony. Because our culture offers scant opportunity to experience many of these primary satisfactions, we substitute with secondary satisfactions, of which money and material possessions top the list. The oft-discussed hedonic treadmill is testament to this issue. We ask money and material possessions to address needs they're not designed to address. We experience a burst of dopamine and a short-term bump in happiness when we make a purchase or receive a raise/promotion, but unless that money is specifically used in alignment with our deeper needs and values (of which primary satisfactions usually top the list), the rise in happiness is typically short-lived, and we wind up craving more.

Just as the previous exercise asked you to look at your assumptions about what money was going to "get you," this exercise is about exploring that which really creates an experience of wealth, abundance, and profound contentment for you. Use the prompts here to explore what truly drives you and whether you're aligning your monetary resources with these deeper values and needs.

Reflect back on your happiest moments this past year (or two if a longer time horizon is helpful). What were they?

1. _____

2. _____

3. _____

Looking at this list, what values/needs were met during these moments? What words would you use to describe your internal experience during these moments (these might help you identify your deeper values/needs)? Were these moments of primary or secondary satisfactions?

_____

_____

_____

_____

What role, if any, did money play in experiencing these moments?

_____

_____

_____

_____

If you were to align your relationship to money with what you are learning truly satisfies you, what would be different? How would you spend your money differently, and how would you allocate your time in terms of its acquisition?

_____

_____

_____

Expansion Move 6: Flip Your Negativity Bias

When we use the lens of scarcity to relate to money, our attention goes to where we need/want more. We focus on deficiency rather than sufficiency. We tend to think of the sin of greed as related to money and financial resources. However, we can bring the lens of scarcity to any need or resource of ours that we value, not just money. We can be greedy and believe we don't have enough intimacy, connection, time, energy, rest, love, support, and so on. Just as the scarcity mindset with respect to money exists independent from the facts of how much money we actually have, the same is true for all that we value. We can choose to experience scarcity or sufficiency in all realms of our lives. With respect to money, but also with respect to what we more deeply value—your broader resources and your deeper needs—this expansion move is about cultivating a lens of sufficiency, focusing on what we already have and where there is already enough. The antidote to scarcity is appreciation, and appreciation is about noticing how much the present moment is actually filled with everything we are longing for. Practicing appreciation can be done specifically with respect to money, or it can be done with respect to anything else we value and find important. Whether you choose money, time, love, or something else, close your eyes and say out loud, "I have enough _____." Notice what happens in your body, your heart, and your mind when you say this statement out loud. Next, see if you're able to identify three specific, real-time examples in support of the statement "I have enough _____." List those three examples below.

I have enough _____.

Three examples in support of this statement:

1. _____

2. _____

3. _____

How do you feel, and what do you notice when you deliberately shift your lens away from scarcity to one of sufficiency?

You can bring an orientation of appreciation to your daily life as well. When you catch yourself thinking, "Ugh, I don't have enough [money, time, support]," the practice is to pause and deliver the antidote. Would you be willing to find three concrete examples to the contrary? This appreciation practice also works well when practiced in relationships, whether personal or professional. Rather than ending a team meeting or presentation with what could have gone better, first start by appreciating what went well.

Many of us fear that if we appreciate what we already have or what is going well, we'll lose our motivation to continue to work hard. Many of us fear that if we believe we have enough, we'll lose our "drive" to do anything at all. This has not been our experience, and we invite you to run this experiment and see what happens.

Expansion Move 7: Conduct Some True
Accounting and Distinguish Material Wants from Needs

Elise here. After I left my big corporate gig at the beginning of COVID, I was in a panic about my ability to support my family without the typical structure of a job. Beginning at the age of fourteen, I had always worked for *someone* and had never relied solely on myself. Shortly after, I was on a call with Carissa Schumacher, a psychic medium who is one of the spiritual teachers in my life. Obviously, I wanted her to tell me I would be *just fine*.

"I'm in a panic," I explained. "I don't think I'll have enough."

She slowed me down. "Okay, what do you need?"

"What do you mean, what do I need?"

"Exactly that," she countered. "The universe is very good at meeting needs. But if you don't know what you need because you're swimming in anxiety about 'enough,' then no needs can be met."

"Okay," I offered. "But how do I know what I need?"

"You write it down."

"Like a budget?"

"Sure, but more like a list of needs. You can make a separate list of wants. The universe doesn't really care what you materially want, but it does care about needs."

I've never made a budget—not because I'm not paying attention, but because I pay so much attention; creating a fixed spending plan for myself has always felt like a trigger for more anxiety, particularly with life's curveballs. But I dutifully opened Excel and started filling it out with two sheets: Needs and Wants.

Here's what I found: My needs were significant—mortgage, car payments, power and water, education, childcare, and so on—but as I tabulated the total, it was a number I could get my arms around and set about practically addressing. Meanwhile, I realized that I didn't have many wants despite all the ideas flooding my feed—*Wouldn't it be nice to buy that cozy sweater advertised to me on Instagram?* What I wanted was a couple of family vacations to Montana and Maine and some leeway on takeout. Again, a number I realized I could meet.

I calmed the F down. Once I had a number to get my arms around—a number that I rounded up for emergencies—I had a value for "enough." It also gave me a repeatable process for my wants. Anytime I think I want something material, I write it down. Then I come back to it in a week. Still a want? Or more like a fleeting impulse? It's slowed me down enough to give me a chance to think more deeply about what I buy.

You can do this in Excel or on a piece of paper, but I highly recommend this exercise—even if you have no anxiety about needs, do it for your material wants. Then ask yourself: Do I really want that? How will I feel about this item the day after I purchase it? Can I imagine myself finding ongoing joy in its presence, or will the joy fade immediately after acquisition? Do you want the item or experience in question more than what you already have? Try to put yourself right there, in the moment, and sense into how you'll feel.

NEEDS: _____

WANTS: _____

Expansion Move 8: Worth Versus Value

We often conflate and synonymize value and worth, but they have two very different energies. Here's the distinction from *On Our Best Behavior:* "Worth is an exterior validation: the world deciding what you deserve, your corresponding status. Worth is equivalent to what something costs, including your time. Value, on the other hand, is an internal calculation; it is much more profound, personal. It's the importance of something to you, specifically." An easy example is to think of something you hold priceless: maybe a last letter from a loved one before they passed, a drawing from one of your kids, or a piece of jewelry from your mother that's not precious—but irreplaceably dear. Someone sifting through your things might count these as "worth-less" because they lack market value.

The goal of this internal inquisition is to determine what you value about yourself and how those gifts show up in the world—irrespective of their "worth" in the market. What is invaluable to you? Another way to think about this question is: If we lived in a world without money, where everyone participated in the economy by sharing their primary or core gift—the thing that you value in yourself and loved ones value in you—what would this be? Where do you find the most joy, ease, and flow? (Hint: It should be a creative task, not, say, watching TV.)

Elise here, but I use this as a tool when I think about the projects I take on: While money is always a factor for me—particularly because I'm scarce on time—I don't say yes to anything unless it's something I would theoretically be pleased to do for free. Because of this rigor (see Expansion Moves 3 through 6 in Sloth, as I always run everything through my body), there is nothing on my docket that I'm not legitimately excited to engage in and where I don't feel like I can bring unique value—and no, I don't work for free. Perhaps this is a luxury, but I don't think of it that way: I would be far richer if I said yes to everything, but I'd be way more miserable and infinitely more drained.

Expansion Move 9: Become More Candid About Money

Elise here. Many years ago, I met Sallie Krawcheck, the CEO of Ellevest, for a drink. Krawcheck, the onetime CEO of Smith Barney who had earned the moniker "the Most Powerful Woman on Wall Street," is dead set on bridging the wealth gap for women—and getting women more comfortable talking about money, particularly because we're so good with it.

"How much do you make?" she asked.

I answered her directly, and she almost fell off her chair. "You're one of the first women to answer that question directly," she told me. The programming to "never talk about money" runs deep, and most of us are ashamed to break this social taboo, convinced that we either have or make too much money—or that we don't, and should be equally ashamed. But to Krawcheck's point, the less we talk about money, the more we ensure these narratives stick around. So here's our task: We have to become more candid about money and start *talking about it, all the time.* Does this make you shudder? All the more reason to push through. You can practice this in several ways. You can put together a brain trust with women who are in your industry and openly discuss financial metrics—compensation, bonus structure, equity plans. None of us benefit from a lack of transparency around compensation—I've accidentally been given access to confidential compensation information three times in my career because of a clerical error, and I was *never* happy with what I saw. I'd been taking the party line at face value that my salary was in line with my peers'. Turns out that wasn't true. It's also worth risking candor with men—I've had several male mentors and bosses who have championed me in negotiating for myself and have given me deeper insight into market trends.

As people who work for ourselves, Courtney and I talk about our rates a lot—particularly because we deliver these rates directly to clients (in her case, individuals; in mine, corporations). I've spent a lot of time with Courtney and other freelance friends comparing rates and work scopes—not to mimic what other people charge but to ground our confidence in research and reality. Nobody has ever asked me to defend my ask—though I easily could. But by creating firm parameters for myself, I'm able to offer rates without caveats. I've coached many women out of offering to negotiate as they send off their first proposal (e.g., "I can be flexible"). No. This doesn't mean that you can't be flexible, but you don't start by suggesting you should be talked down.

In the personal realm, it can be touchy to talk about money—particularly if there's a wide range of income and net worth within your friend group. This doesn't mean that you should politely sweep these types of conversation under the rug. It can be, frankly, incredibly relieving to set levels of spending with your friends, particularly if their style of travel or taste in restaurants is not within reach for you. Because these conversations feel scary for many of us, start by admitting that you feel scared to even broach the conversation. Name what your fears are, specifically. Even just naming the fear or concern ends up drawing you closer in your friendship and then, whatever specific circumstances you are trying to negotiate, getting them resolved relatively easily.

Expansion Move 10: End Your Complicity

Take personal responsibility for our cultural judgments of women and money. We are just as much active creators in our culture as anyone else. As we've been exploring throughout this chapter, the experience of wealth or its absence and the labels of rich and poor are more complicated than we might initially think. Notice when you find yourself defaulting to attributing greater or lesser value to yourself or to others based on financial status. Catch when you have internal or voiced judgments about what people with a certain amount of financial resources should or should not be doing. Make a commitment with your friends to voice these stories out loud, not with the intention of gossiping but with the goal of complicating the dominant narratives about money that we have inherited and, most likely, perpetuate.

6

LUST

Do you allow yourself to feel pleasure?

WHAT YOU'LL RECOVER: ACCESS TO A DEEPER RELATIONSHIP WITH YOUR BODY AND THE SOURCE OF YOUR CREATIVE ENERGY

The etymology of *creature* and *creative* comes from *creare* (Latin): "form out of nothing." Women, in particular, understand this capacity: We can make entire people, entire worlds, with our bodies. One glance at our patriarchal culture's ongoing insistence on controlling our procreative ability gives you a sense of how terrifying these abilities are to some men. In many ways, women have the power of God. This agency to create doesn't begin and end with children either: We all—men too, obviously—have the ability to originate new ideas, concepts, systems, and ways of being in the world. It's a stunning gift.

Our fertility, our sexual function, and our desirability receive a lot of attention—as does our ability to give birth. This gift for women is a heavy load: In our culture, where a premium is placed on our appearance and our ability to compel attention, we're also tasked with keeping ourselves safe. Be attractive, but whatever you attract is therefore your problem. There are no true victims in a sexual assault; the blame often comes to land back on us: *But what were you wearing? How many drinks did you have? Why did you get into the Uber? Did you fight back . . . adequately and thoroughly?*

For this reason, when mothers ask me for advice about their daughters' choice of dress, I struggle for the right response: I don't want to body- or slut-shame anyone, and yet we don't live in a world that's protective of girls and women. These girls and women will be held accountable for their crop tops and whale tail bikinis should harm come their way. After all, girls are set up as the more responsible party, the babysitters to the rapacious sexual desires of boys and men. It's on us to patrol the edges of our bodies, to ensure our own security. In many ways, this can feel like a fool's errand.

The "Lust" chapter in *On Our Best Behavior* was one of the most difficult to write, as it required an excavation of my own checkered sexual past, marked by a garden variety of events in childhood and early adulthood. After all, a vast majority of girls—and many, many boys—are victims of sexual assault and abuse, which colors the way they experience their sexuality going forward. For me, attention from men is commingled with threat and danger: I don't enjoy it, nor do I want it. Or at least, that's one of the stories that I tell myself to keep myself safe.

Sex is also complicated by the very basic reality of libido—and hormones that fluctuate throughout our lives. This isn't helped by a culture that puts the focus on quantity of sexual encounters rather than quality: When it comes to sexual education in our schools, we definitely don't talk to kids about pleasure or asking for what you want or for what feels good—and for girls, we stress their capacity to provide pleasure to boys while skipping over what will feel good for them. Journalist Peggy Orenstein, who writes prodigiously about sex and kids, calls this the "American psychological clitoridectomy." While in Denmark, parents coach "responsibility and joy," Americans are more likely to preach "risk and danger."

All of this leaves us with many different stories about sexuality: *I need to keep myself pure and clean, Sexiness is my primary value, I'm a prude! I love my body and making it feel good,* and on, and on, and on. In this domain, our stories vary—some of us have no hang-ups, many of us have a lot.

I often wonder if my wariness of sexual energy is ingrained or learned. Dipping into the Enneagram for a minute, Courtney would coach that there's something to be learned from what are called Instincts. I'm passing the torch to her for a brief Enneagram intermission:

The Enneagram is most commonly known as a system that categorizes human beings into one of nine types. Each type is preoccupied with a particular human need (e.g., freedom, value, love, integrity), and each type develops a habitual set of traits, feelings, and thought patterns constellated around this need. However, the Enneagram also looks at what lies underneath these nine basic personality types: the Instincts or basic biological drives that all humans come preloaded with as animals. You can see some form of the Instincts in all living creatures, and in the system of the Enneagram, we group these Instincts into three categories: **Self-Preservation, Social, and Sexual.** *(While the study of the Instincts has long been part of the Enneagram tradition, there has been renewed interest in this aspect of the Enneagram with the publication of John Luckovich's recent book* The Instinctual Drives and the Enneagram. *We are relying upon a short summary of his work here.)*

Each person has a sequence or "stack" of these Instincts. The first Instinct in our personal sequence is considered dominant, meaning we distort its needs and overemphasize its way of relating to the world. We tend to have a more neutral relationship to the Instinct that is second in our sequence. With the Instinct that is last in our "stack," we tend to overlook its needs and can often experience disgust or judgment when we're around others who prioritize this Instinct. In the language of the Enneagram, we say that the last Instinct in our sequence is repressed and that we are "blind" to it. Therefore, for those of us who have the Sexual Instinct last in our instinctual stacking, we feel threatened by its energy, and we fear what may happen if we acknowledge ourselves as sexual beings. For those of us who have the Sexual Instinct first in our instinctual stacking, we tend to exaggerate its importance to our way of being in the world.

The Self-Preservation Instinct *is the easiest to understand. It's this: "I'm driven to ensure that I survive, which shows up as prioritizing and attending to my hunger and fatigue. I have a natural desire to secure resources, skills, a home, et cetera." In nature, imagine a plant—one like a cactus that can store water, and also the image of a flower cracking a sidewalk to reach light and air. Our incredible resilience under dire circumstances is a function of the Self-Preservation Instinct. Over time, we can lose touch with our actual needs—we come to believe that spiritual needs can be met through securing these biological needs. I would argue that in capitalism we frequently see the Self-Preservation Instinct gone massively awry, where we've lost connection to what our body actually needs for its survival and growth.*

The **Social Instinct** *rides on the fundamental need for approval: We need tribe to survive. We've developed many biological drives that ensure we pay attention to how we are perceived by others, to whether our social position is secure, and to whether we belong. The Social Instinct is why many of us participate in team sports, build community, and self-sacrifice on behalf of others. It is the source of altruism and why moms instinctually sacrifice* *themselves for their children as well. This Instinct is most commonly seen in mammals, animals who devote disproportionate resources to caring for their children, although other species, including even some trees, also have complex social networks and self-sacrifice for the benefit of the whole. However, just as the Self-Preservation Instinct can become distorted and overdone, we can have an unhealthy relationship to the Social Instinct as well. We can overdo our need to belong, and we become willing to conform to tribe, no matter the cost.*

*Finally, the **Sexual Instinct** is a fascinating biological drive. We commonly understand it as the need to propagate the species, but from an evolutionary perspective it needed to be strong enough to overcome the Self-Preservation Instinct, which would potentially cause you to revolt against the idea of accepting foreign material into your body. The Sexual Instinct as an evolutionary drive is classically defined by the peacock, an animal that devotes a lot of resources to sexual display rather than its self-preservation. Those with high Sexual Instinct feel a drive toward chemistry, electricity, change, transformation, union, and general agitation. They have a drive toward attraction and differentiation rituals. The primary focus of individuals with the Sexual Instinct as dominant is achieving the high that comes from feeling attraction. When you encounter someone with a strong Sexual Instinct, they often believe they are also meeting their spiritual needs through the biological experience of sexual chemistry. For those of us whose Sexual Instinct comes last in our sequence, we might experience others with a different orientation to their sexual drive as living, walking sex organs, exuding sexuality irrespective of target.*

Therefore, in the tradition of the Enneagram, each person identifies as one of nine personality types, and each person also has a particular instinctual sequence. Our type and instinctual stacking intersect with one another, and, no matter our type, we begin to conflate the fundamental human need that our type focuses on (e.g., freedom, love, value, harmony) with the biological needs represented by the Instincts. This is one way that we develop a distorted relationship with our Instincts. We begin to believe that our deeper human needs are met when our self-preservation, social, or sexual needs are met, rather than understanding them to be distinct aspects of our humanity. Elise and I are both Type 6's, so I'll use that breakdown here as an example. Because all Type 6's seek to feel guided and supported in their navigation of reality:

- ***Self-Preservation 6****: They believe they will experience a sense of support and guidance by amassing resources to ensure their physical survival.*

- *Social 6:* They believe they will experience a sense of support and guidance by knowing their position in the community.
- *Sexual 6:* They believe they will experience a sense of support and guidance by turning on, controlling, or locking into the current of sexual chemistry with someone else.

Through this lens, all three Instincts can drive a desire to engage in sexual intimacy. Often unconsciously, people have sex for different reasons, all of which are expressions of our basic biological drives:

- *Self-Preservation:* "I'm in a (somewhat) transactional relationship with my partner where I offer sexual availability in exchange for material resources."
- *Social:* "I use sex to find intimacy, emotional connection, and belonging in partnership."
- *Sexual:* "I use sex to feel 'turned on,' alive, and full of magnetism and electricity."

Elise here, but as a Social 6, followed by Self-Preservation, I am sexually "blind," which means that it makes me incredibly uncomfortable when people present me with their sexual energy—it is not how I'm comfortable interacting with the world. Like most women, I've experienced my share of sexual trauma that I continue to contend with (I write about this in *On Our Best Behavior*), but learning about the Sexual Instinct (or its lack thereof) has been eye-opening for me and has caused me some relief. Rather than feeling that something is "wrong with me" because sexual attention makes me uncomfortable, I've come to understand that it's not my trauma talking necessarily, it's just not my primary language or means for contacting that world. Learning this has allowed me to cut myself some slack and to recognize that this in no way inhibits me from getting in touch with the creative energy that runs through the same channels. I've also come to understand that there are many ways to feel "turned on" and that this is very rarely about sex for me but more likely about feeling intellectually or emotionally stimulated.

Thanks to the culture that we live in, there's a good chance that your relationship to sexuality and creativity is complicated, whether you've experienced trauma or not. Lust is a sin with major cultural imprinting, but it is also one of the sins that overlaps with our instinctual needs as human beings, a sin where each of us tries to negotiate being both an animal and a creature of spirit. (Sloth, gluttony, and greed are the others.) When we work with the sin of lust, we are not merely exploring our relationship to sexual intimacy, we are owning our birthright to experience pleasure, attraction, sexual chemistry, and creative potential in all aspects of our life.

CORE PROCESS APPLIED TO THE SIN OF LUST
Tool 1: Is It a Fact or Is It a Story?
Excavating Unconscious Stories

For a full explanation of this tool, see page 10.

First, brainstorm some facts relevant to your relationship to sexuality and pleasure. We've offered some examples below.

FACTS ABOUT LUST

Elise Example: I lost my virginity when I was seventeen.

Courtney Example: I am forty-eight years old and experiencing some of the symptoms of perimenopause.

YOUR FACTS:

1. _____

2. _____

3. _____

Tip: Are these facts capable of being documented by a video recorder? For example, "I've slept with thirteen people" is a fact. "I should have slept with more" is a story.

Second, brainstorm the stories that you make up about these facts.

STORIES I MAKE UP ABOUT LUST

Elise's Fact 1:

I lost my virginity when I was seventeen.

Stories Elise makes up about that fact:

This was the "right" age.

I needed to be in love with my boyfriend.

Nobody could judge me or have an opinion about losing my virginity to him because it was "appropriate."

Courtney's Fact 1:

I am forty-eight years old and experiencing some of the symptoms of perimenopause.

Stories Courtney makes up about that fact:

I have only a few years left before my interest in sex disappears.

As I age, fewer men will flirt with me and find me attractive.

I should delay the onset of menopause as long as I can.

Fact 1: _____

Stories you make up about that fact: _____

_____

_____

Fact 2: _____

Stories you make up
about that fact: _____

_____

_____

Fact 3: _____

Stories you make up
about that fact: _____

_____

_____

Third, use the questions below to help you brainstorm some of the additional stories you have about lust.

- What stories do you make up about your sexual history?
- What stories do you make up about your partner's sexual history?
- What stories do you make up about naming and acting on your sexual desires?
- What stories do you make up about experiencing pleasure?
- What stories do you make up about women who are frank about their sexuality?
- What stories do you make up about girls and women who dress in "provocative" ways?

Elise Examples:

- Women who are highly sexual scare the shit out of me because they add an energy to encounters that makes me feel uncomfortable.
- "I don't want to see it." I often wish women and girls would put on more clothing.

- My husband has a lot more sexual experience than I do and he's probably really bored by me.

Courtney Examples:

- Sexuality is a fundamental aspect of being human.
- My kids shouldn't have access to songs like "WAP" (Wet-Ass Pussy) by Cardi B. featuring Megan Thee Stallion; their performance at the Grammy Awards was inappropriate for television.
- People who can't control their sexual desires often ruin their lives and hurt others.

YOUR STORIES:

1. _____

2. _____

3. _____

4. _____

5. _____

Now that you've excavated some of the stories that underlie your relationship to sexuality and pleasure, go back through what you've written and star the two or three that drive you the most. Those are the stories that we recommend working with throughout the rest of this chapter.

Tool 2: And Then What?

Tracing the Acting, Sensing, Feeling, and Thinking Loop

For a full description of this tool, see page 13.

Take the first story you want to work with from your starred list. You can repeat this process as many times as you want with different stories.

Story: _____

Step 1: What Actions Do You Take?

When I choose to believe this story, this is how I show up in the world:

My behaviors are: _____

I start to prioritize: _____

My attention goes to: _____

Three specific examples where I notice this story driving my behavior are:

When I: _____

When I: _____

When I: _____

Step 2: What Sensations Do You Feel?

When I choose to believe this story, I experience the following sensations in my body:

In my forehead, I feel:

Swirling	Fogginess	Buzziness
Spaciousness	Density	Sharpness
Scattered	Throbbing	Stirred up

In the back of my neck, across my shoulders, and in my jaw, I feel:

Tight	Twisted	Pulling
Bunched	Itchy	Burning
Cord-like	Clenched	Steely
Rigid	Blocky	Prickly

Across my high chest and upper throat, I feel:

Heaviness	Constriction	Cut off
Closed in	Numb	Melting
Compressed	Achy	Pierced
Unable to breathe	Flatness	Cold

Around the stomach area, I feel:

Knotted	Fluttering	Butterflies
Nauseous	Braced	Hollow
Churning	Empty	Doubled-over

In other parts of my body, I feel:

Racing heart	Trembling hands	Low-energy
Collapsed	Wiggly	Teary
Expanded	Tingly	Stretched

These tables are adapted from Gay and Katie Hendricks's work on body sensations and intelligence. See www.hendricks.com for further information.

Step 3: What Feelings Do You Have?

When I choose to believe this story, I experience the following emotions:

Anger

LOW	MEDIUM	HIGH
Annoyed	Agitated	Enraged
Bored	Disgusted	Furious
Bothered	Frustrated	Hostile
Dissatisfied	Indignant	Livid
Irritable	Irritated	Outraged
Tense	Resentful	Vengeful

Sadness

LOW	MEDIUM	HIGH
Blue	Discouraged	Agony
Down	Gloomy	Anguished
Lonely	Hopeless	Devastated
Somber	Melancholic	Heartbroken
Solemn	Regretful	Grief-stricken
Unhappy	Sorrowful	Mourning

Fear

LOW	MEDIUM	HIGH
Concerned	Apprehensive	Frightened
Guarded	Edgy	Frozen
Hesitant	Jumpy	Panicked
Reluctant	Nervous	Petrified
Suspicious	Startled	Shocked
Vulnerable	Worried	Terrified

Joy

LOW	MEDIUM	HIGH
Calm	Cheerful	Blissful
Carefree	Excited	Delighted
Content	Graceful	Ecstatic
Lighthearted	Optimistic	Enthusiastic
Peaceful	Proud	Elated
Relaxed	Thankful	Expansive

These tables are excerpted with permission from the Conscious Leadership Group's work on emotions. See www.conscious.is for further information.

Step 4: What Thoughts Come Next?

When I choose to believe this story, the following thoughts arise:

I begin to think that: _____

I judge myself as: _____

I judge others [insert name] as: _____

Tool 3: Why Stories Stick

Identifying the Underlying Fear

For a full description of this tool and the corresponding "Flavors of Fear" chart, see page 22.

Take one of the stories that you excavated in Tool 1 and explored in Tool 2. We're now going to investigate the fear activated by this particular story.

You can repeat this exercise for as many stories as you wish.

On pages 215 to 216, we have included examples of this process using our own stories.

Story: _____

When I believe this story and consider the actions, body sensations, emotions, and thinking patterns that it generates, what flavor(s) of fear does it most directly map onto?

- Fight
- Flee
- Freeze
- Fawn
- Faint

Tip: If this exercise feels difficult for you, you might consider standing up, repeating your story aloud a few times, and exaggerating the posture your body takes on as you go into the story.

If I were to disregard this story, what am I afraid might happen?

_____

What am I *really* afraid might happen?

_____

Tip: You may need to ask the question "What am I *really* afraid might happen?" a few times in order to get at the root fear that is activated. There is no wrong answer here, just an intention to understand and be with your own experience a bit more.

Does that fear seem most related to:

- A loss of control?
- A loss of approval?
- A loss of security?

As you sit with what you've learned, see if you'd be willing to acknowledge and accept that there is a part of you that feels scared. The goal is to be with this fear rather than pushing it away.

EXAMPLES:

> Elise's Story: Nobody could judge me or have an opinion about me losing my virginity to him because it was "appropriate."

Fear Flavor: Fight or Freeze

If I were to disregard this story, what am I afraid might happen?

People would talk about me and call me a slut.

What am I *really* afraid might happen?

That boys would decide I was an "easy" target and I wouldn't be able to protect myself—and that anything that happened to me would be my fault because of my reputation.

This fear is most related to: Security

> Courtney's Story: I have only a few years left before my interest in sex disappears.

Fear Flavor: Fight and Faint

If I were to disregard this story, what am I afraid might happen?

I would have to acknowledge that sexual desire is not something I can control and anticipate and plan for.

What am I *really* afraid might happen?

I would have to acknowledge that the effects of aging are not something I can control. I would have to acknowledge that I actually have no idea what my sexual desires will look like in a few years.

This fear is most related to: Control

Tool 4: Welcome to the Drama Triangle
Relating to Stories from Victimhood Consciousness

Story: _____

For a comprehensive explanation of the Drama Triangle, see page 27.

Pick a specific situation in which this story shows up in your life (see the specific examples you listed in Tool 2 for the story you're working with).

Rotate through the three positions of the Drama Triangle and answer the following questions with respect to this situation/story.

You can write your answers down in this workbook and/or use this tool as an opportunity to stand up and voice your answers out loud. Either way, this is not the time to be polite. The Victim, Villain, and Hero all see reality through overly simplified and reductionist lenses. When you take on their voices, we encourage you to use raw and simple language. Write or speak plainly. No one else is reading this material. It's here for you and you alone. We even dare you to have fun.

THE VICTIM LENS

How are you hurt, taken advantage of, or burdened?

_____

What do you find yourself worrying about over and over again?

_____

Where do you feel overwhelmed, helpless, or ineffectual?

_____

In what ways do you feel that life is unfair?

_____

THE VILLAIN LENS

Who do you blame, hold responsible, or see as the enemy?

_____

What beliefs do you have 100 percent certainty about?

_____

What/who needs to do something different to fix this situation?

_____

What do you take very seriously?

_____

THE HERO LENS

How do you ensure you are needed?

_____

Where do you take on responsibilities that are not yours?

_____

What are you avoiding or suppressing?

_____

How do you minimize or distract yourself from any discomfort?

_____

REFLECTION

Which role in the Drama Triangle feels the most familiar to you?

_____

What are you most afraid of?

_____

What have you not yet fully faced or accepted about this situation?

_____

What truths or feelings have you not yet expressed about this situation?

_____

Tool 5: What Do These Stories Get You?
Owning the Payoffs and Costs of Our Unconscious Stories

Story: _____

Who taught me this story?

_____

What do I gain from believing this story?

_____

In what way does believing this story serve me?

_____

Who do I get to stay close with by believing this story?

_____

How do I keep this story going?

_____

If I didn't believe this story, what would I be doing instead?

_____

What does this story cost me?

_____

If I discard this story, what do I have to risk?

_____

How do I use this story to keep me from devoting my energy to that which makes me feel truly alive?

_____

In order to discard this story, what role, behavior, or way of being do I need to shed and grow out of?

_____

How would my relationship to myself change if I didn't believe this story?

_____

How would my relationship to [insert name] change if I didn't believe this story?

_____

These questions are adapted with permission from the Conscious Leadership Group's work on the Drama Triangle. See www.conscious.is for further information.

Tool 6: Teach the Class

Reclaiming Responsibility and Becoming the Creator

Story: _____

Remember: You're teaching this class at a women's college, and you want these twenty-somethings to buy into the exact same story that you are working with here. Your students need very specific instructions that they can follow to re-create and live by this story in their own lives. **The advice that you offer to your students should be actions, feelings, thoughts, and beliefs that they themselves can choose and have control over.** Really commit! Win that teaching prize!

Answer the questions that follow to help you create a game plan for your students:

What actions do you take or not take to ensure you keep believing this story?

_____

What other stories, beliefs, or thoughts should you have about yourself, others, or the world in order to keep this story going?

_____

What feelings should you repress or conceal so that this story remains the same?

_____

What do you withhold and from whom?

_____

What do you try to control that you actually can't?

_____

What do you need to believe you are right about?

_____

What agreements do you have to make and/or break with yourself or with others?

_____

What matters the most to you?

_____

What do you need to feel afraid of losing?

_____

What other "shoulds" do you need to believe?

_____

Now that you have reflected on the specific ways you have ensured that this particular story remains integral in your life, what are you willing to take responsibility for and do differently?

_____

The "Teach the Class" exercise is excerpted with permission from the Conscious Leadership Group's work on personal responsibility. See www.conscious.is for further information.

Tool 7: Playing with Personas

Inviting All Parts of You to the Table

For a full description of this tool, see page 40.

When you believe the stories you have about lust, what persona shows up and dictates your way of being in the world?

EXAMPLES:

> Cleavage Cop Claudia: I judge other women for wearing revealing clothing, for dancing suggestively, or for otherwise acting provocatively.

> It's Not About Me Imogene: If someone is interested in me, I have trouble knowing whether I'm interested in them. I sometimes have sex out of obligation or because I have trouble saying no. I don't ask for what would feel good to me.

> No Bod Below the Belt Barb: I have little interest or time for sexual pleasure. My body is here to get stuff done, not to feel good. I'm in my head so much that I am disconnected from my body's desires.

YOUR PERSONAS:

Name and description: _____

Name and description: _____

GET TO KNOW YOUR PERSONA

Once you have a name for the persona who shows up when you believe your stories about lust, answer the following questions:

In what situations does this persona tend to show up?

_____

What are some classic phrases this persona often says or thinks?

_____

What behaviors and actions are typical for this persona?

_____

Think of a specific situation when this persona recently showed up, and allow him/her to directly answer the following questions:

What is the most important thing to you?

_____

How do you make [insert your own name]'s life better?

_____

When did you first make your appearance?

_____

Who did you learn your style from?

_____

What are you most afraid of?

_____

What do you most want?

_____

These questions are excerpted with permission from *Centering and the Art of Intimacy Handbook*, by Gay and Katie Hendricks. See www.hendricks.com for further information.

THE PAYOFFS AND COSTS OF THIS PERSONA

When I adopt this persona,

I don't have to feel:

_____

I get to be right and make _____ wrong.

I get to control:

_____

I get to avoid:

_____

I get to feel safe by:

_____

But when I adopt this persona,

I don't get to try out:

_____

I don't get to enjoy:

_____

I lose the opportunity to:

_____

I lose this aspect of my humanity:

_____

Expansion Moves for the Sin of Lust

If you could wipe out the influences of your family, culture, and past and instead approach your relationship to your sexuality with fresh eyes, how would you act? What would you do and what would you believe? These expansion moves are designed to help you hit refresh and explore with curiosity and openness what you actually want your relationship to your body's sexuality—and creativity overall—to be. For more on these expansion moves, see page 44.

Expansion Move 1: Tune into and Name the Sensations of Arousal and Attraction

Many of us have been taught to think about arousal as a set of biological sensations caused by our sexual attraction to another person. However, we can be attracted to, lit up by, electrified, or magnetized by all sorts of activities, people, and experiences. Being "turned on" doesn't necessarily mean that we're interested in sexual activity. Rather, it signifies more broadly that something or someone is drawing us in, producing an experience so heightened that we feel transformed, consumed, and more alive. Because our culture conflates attraction and arousal with sexual activity, many of us have lost awareness of when we feel turned on, and we have learned to downplay and not express when we feel electrified, aroused, or attracted to someone or something.

This practice is about tuning in and listening for the moments when we feel attraction rising in our body and then identifying and naming these sensations, rather than judging and suppressing them. As Elise and I have become comfortable with this practice, we have found that we're attracted to all kinds of experiences, people, and activities and that these biological sensations arise throughout the course of a day. When we're willing to name and fully experience attraction in the body, we reclaim a fundamental and highly pleasurable part of what it means to be human. We also reconnect with the intelligence baked into attraction. It points to when and where we feel fully alive and when and where we're feeling a desire to express our creative and generative capacities.

For this practice, we invite you first to identify the body sensations that signal to you that you're drawn in, lit up by, or attracted to someone/something. Is it a warm, liquidy feeling? Where do you feel it in the body? Does a particular part of your body flush? Do you experience tingly sensations anywhere? Does your body feel larger or smaller than it usually does, and do you sense your energy rising or falling? What is happening with your heart rate or breath?

Just as you would with an emotion, we now invite you to label the sensations of arousal/attraction that you're experiencing in the body. We've included suggested language from the Conscious Leadership Group to get you started. As you pay attention to and name the sensations of attraction, we also invite you to notice whether any judgments or stories arise in your mind, all of which are ripe material for you to use with the core process outlined in this workbook. We recommend that you commit to using this practice regularly for a period of time and to notice how you might relate to yourself differently as you become more willing to acknowledge the sexual intelligence of your body.

Suggested Words to Describe the Experience of Attraction

LOW	MEDIUM	HIGH
Aroused	Glowing	Enthralled
Attracted	Excited	Euphoric
Interested	Gleeful	Intoxicated
Inspired	Hot	Orgasmic
Stimulated	Passionate	Prolific
Tickled	Sensual	Rapturous

This table is excerpted with permission from the Conscious Leadership Group's work on emotions. See www.conscious.is for further information.

Expansion Move 2: Trust and Translate the Signals of Attraction/Arousal

One reason many of us are uncomfortable naming when we feel attracted to or aroused by someone/something is that we have concerns about what this arousal may mean for our primary relationship. Many of us are scared to acknowledge when someone or something turns us on because we believe this attraction is inappropriate, disloyal, betraying, or threatening. That said, just as we reframed envy not as an uncomfortable, petty, or negative emotion but as a feeling that points to what we want, we can reframe attraction/arousal. Instead of it being an uncontrollable or threatening sensation, it is a clue pointing to how we'd like to create more aliveness in our existing relationships. Rather than impulsively acting on the sensation or suppressing the feeling for fear of acting impulsively, when someone/something attracts us, we can trust that the attraction points to what we'd like to cultivate more of in our existing lives.

Noticing that we're attracted to/aroused by someone or something is an opportunity to pause and inquire as to just what quality is attracting us in the first place. Is it novelty, unfamiliarity, mystery, surprise? Is it playfulness and flirtation? Is it intensity and intimacy? Is it wildness and unpredictability? How do you feel when you're around this person or in this experience? Sexier and more free?

More relaxed and in your body? Creative and abundant? Once we've identified the attribute or vibe that we're attracted to rather than just the person or experience who happens to embody it, we can become curious about how we can deliberately invite that quality into our existing relationships and priorities. This practice invites us to trust that feelings of attraction/arousal are important signals our body uses to tell us what we'd like more of, pointing to where we feel constricted and stagnant rather than fully alive.

Expansion Move 3: Take Responsibility for Your Own Turn-On

Often, when we describe when we're feeling aroused or turned on, we attribute it to what is going on outside of ourselves—a particular person entering the room, or something our partner does or says to us. When we outsource the origin of arousal to individuals, activities, or environments outside of us, we are inadvertently relating to attraction as something that happens *to us* rather than an attitude or a way of being in the world that we are responsible for creating. The goal of this practice is to reclaim responsibility for whether we're cultivating a willingness to be turned on by life, rather than blaming our external conditions for whether we feel aroused or sexually inclined. Whether we're in a committed relationship or not, whether we're having sex as often as we would like or not, this practice invites the realization that we can fully inhabit ourselves as sexual beings independent of these circumstances.

This practice is a repeating-question practice, meaning you will ask yourself the following question: "I turn myself on when I . . ." and then answer this prompt repeatedly. This practice asks you to consider and to take responsibility for when you "turn yourself on" and when you "turn yourself off." You'll know that something turns you on when it produces the bodily sensations of arousal and attraction that you identified in Expansion Move 1 of this chapter. Things you do that "turn yourself off" decrease the chances you will feel these bodily sensations of arousal or attraction. The learning typically emerges, not in the first response, but through what you write as you engage with the question over and over again. We've given you space to answer each question eight times, but feel free to keep going if you like. We've answered the question ourselves to give you an example of what the inquiry looks like as well.

COURTNEY'S EXAMPLES:

I turn myself on when I <u>dance in front of the mirror</u>.

I turn myself on when I <u>play tennis or pickleball or other competitive sports</u>.

I turn myself on when I <u>eat nourishing and healthy food</u>.

I turn myself on when I <u>devote time to coaching or other work requiring my creativity and presence</u>.

I turn myself on when I <u>spend time in the pool or cold plunge</u>.

I turn myself on when I <u>flirt</u>.

I turn myself on when I <u>wear clothing that I feel attractive in</u>.

ELISE'S EXAMPLES:

I turn myself on when I <u>read a great book and feel synapses of connection firing</u>.

I turn myself on when I <u>get really engaged thinking through things with a podcast guest</u>.

I turn myself on when I <u>move fast through nature, whether skiing or riding horses or hiking briskly</u>.

I turn myself on when I <u>tickle my husband's back or hold his hand</u>.

I turn myself on when I <u>laugh a lot at a dinner party or sit next to someone I can really dive deep with</u>.

YOUR RESPONSES:

I turn myself on when I: _____.

I turn myself on when I: _____.

I turn myself on when I: _____.

I turn myself on when I: _____.

I turn myself on when I: _____.

COURTNEY'S EXAMPLES:

I turn myself off when I <u>overeat</u>.

I turn myself off when I <u>don't get enough sleep</u>.

I turn myself off when I <u>spend a lot of time talking about schedules and logistics</u>.

I turn myself off when I <u>focus on my work or my children and deprioritize my own self-care</u>.

I turn myself off when I <u>engage in small talk rather than creating conversations that are playful and engaging</u>.

I turn myself off when I <u>judge my body</u>.

I turn myself off when I <u>read books/articles about perimenopause</u>.

ELISE'S EXAMPLES:

I turn myself off when I <u>realize I've been working all day and have barely gotten up from my desk</u>.

I turn myself off when I <u>cancel too many therapy sessions in a row and feel emotionally overfull</u>.

I turn myself off when I <u>eat foods that make me feel a little ill</u>.

I turn myself off when I <u>say yes to plans that actually feel like a huge no</u>.

I turn myself off when I <u>show up for group activities when I really feel like being alone</u>.

YOUR RESPONSES:

I turn myself off when I: _____.

I turn myself off when I: _____.

I turn myself off when I: _____.

I turn myself off when I: _____.

I turn myself off when I: _____.

Expansion Move 4: Tell the Story of Your Relationship to Your Sexuality

Courtney here. This practice is inspired by an activity I did during a workshop with Esther Perel. Our sexuality is a dynamic aspect of ourselves, which we sometimes lose sight of. The practice is an opportunity to reflect on the ebbs and flows of your relationship to your own sexuality, which you do by breaking your life down into five-year increments and then rating your level of satisfaction with your sexuality during that period. As you do this, jot down some quick notes as to why each period earned its ranking.

Once you've completed this activity, take a step back and look at the overall arc of your evolution as a sexual being. Has there been a trend? (Most people tend to report that satisfaction with their sexuality has improved over time.) Do certain themes or recurring issues emerge? If you were to give a tagline to the overall narrative, or the ever-evolving story, of your own relationship to your own sexuality, what would it be? Notice what emotions, judgments, or stories arise for you as you explore this practice.

AGE	RATING (1–10)	NOTES
Birth–Puberty		
Teen Years		
Early 20s		
Mid-Late 20s		
30s		
40s		
50s		
60s		
70s		

Trends and patterns: _____

_____

_____

Narrative Tagline: _____

Expansion Move 5: Persona Play as a Form of Shadow Integration

We can do a lot with persona play: It's a way to explore parts of ourselves that are underdeveloped, parts of ourselves that "we would never do," parts of ourselves that we admire and feel attracted to in others, and, conversely, parts of ourselves that we judge and feel an aversion to when we see these parts in other people. For more context on playing with shadow personas, refer to the explanation at the end of the chapter "Sloth," on page 67.

Here are some suggested personas in the realm of sexuality and lust that you may judge or have an aversion to. If you find yourself saying "I would never" to any of these characters, that is a sign you may want to inhabit one for a limited time under safe and predefined terms. Pick an evening, whether at home or out, and ask your partner or friends to serve as co-conspirators. You don't have to commit to playing the personas on the regular (unless you want to). That said, the more fully you exaggerate and inhabit the role, the greater the opportunity for loads of laughter and learning.

While persona play is something we recommend in several of the chapters of this workbook, it's a more natural practice with respect to lust given how often many of us already incorporate sexual role play into the bedroom. Whether you're dressing up as Naughty Nurse to fulfill a particular fantasy or channeling any of the personas listed on the next page, persona play in the bedroom works because it creates some distance from your everyday self and allows you to safely explore uncharted territory within yourself. Putting on a costume can take the charge out of saying exactly what you want from your partner, particularly if you've never given voice to this desire before: It lets you triangulate through another entity. While we've been encouraging you *not* to triangulate over the course of this workbook—to really focus on yourself—in this sphere, where we can be shy and nervous, it is okay. It can also be fun—and funny.

SUGGESTED PERSONAS:

Flirty Fiona: I twirl my hair and giggle, and I'm not afraid to act a little dumb. I would *never* buy my own drinks. I love the sparkle and titillation of the chase.

Smutty Sherry: My number one, absolute favorite topic of all time is sex. I'm not ashamed to talk boldly about my own sex life and to ask others about theirs. If I'm really honest, I like the shocked look people give me when they think I've gone too far.

Tantric Tanya: I take every opportunity to make love, whether it's to a beautiful butterfly or a barista. I've been known to break out into spontaneous orgasm due to the level of kundalini energy I naturally run.

Assertive Amanda: I'm super confident, and I both know and ask for what I want. After all, it's a privilege to get to meet my needs.

YOUR PERSONAS:

Name and description: _____

Name and description: _____

Expansion Move 6: The Pleasure of Giving and Receiving

This practice invites you to explicitly explore with your partner or with a friend the pleasures of both giving and receiving. Whether this is something you try with a sexual or nonsexual partner, the objective of the practice is to be intentional about whether you're giving or receiving and whether you're giving or receiving for your pleasure or for someone else's.

With either kind of partner, pick a particular body part where you're going to practice giving or receiving pleasure. You can choose anything from a nonsexual back massage to oral sex, but we suggest you pick a body part/activity where the receiver can fully relax into their role. During this practice, one person will receive and the other person will give, and you will break down the time into two five- or ten-minute intervals. Then you will switch roles and repeat the practice.

If you are the giver, start the practice by focusing solely on the pleasure you are giving to your partner. Pay attention to their nonverbal cues as to what they like. You might ask them what they want more or less of—whether they prefer more or less pressure, a faster or slower pace, et cetera.

After the timer has gone off marking the end of the first interval, set the timer again. The giver will continue to give and the receiver will continue to receive, but this time the giver will focus on giving solely for *their* own pleasure. In what ways does your giving differ when you focus on what your partner likes and then when you focus on what you like? For the receiver, how does the experience differ when the giver focuses on your needs and then their own?

After the timer has gone off for the second time, you switch roles and the giver becomes the receiver and the receiver, the giver. Repeat the practice as described above.

Whether you practice this move with sexual or nonsexual activity, there is so much learning to be gained. What role feels the most natural to you? Does focusing your attention on yourself or on the other feel more natural? As the receiver, was it easy or difficult to describe exactly what you liked? You can repeat this exercise as often as you like and notice what happens when you are explicit about the "why" of touch and how intentionality about role and purpose changes your relationship to giving and receiving pleasure.

Expansion Move 7: End Your Complicity

Take personal responsibility for our cultural judgments of women and our attitudes toward women's sexuality or sexiness. We are just as much active creators in our culture as anyone else. Make a commitment with your friends to end the practice of gossiping about the way women and girls dress or the way they comport themselves sexually. If you catch yourself judging a woman, whether a celebrity, a stranger, or someone in your circle, voice the judgment out loud and use it for your own learning purposes.

1

ANGER

Do you know how to express your boundaries?

WHAT YOU'LL RECOVER: ACCESS TO ALL YOUR EMOTIONS, THE ABILITY TO ESTABLISH LIMITS AND NEEDS, AND THE FREEDOM OF COMPLETE EXPRESSION

We are not kind to angry women in our culture—unless, of course, they're protecting its patriarchal structures (cue Sarah Palin or Phyllis Schlafly). In *On Our Best Behavior*, I attempt to trace the beginning of when women were told to pipe down. Historian Mary Beard offers that in the *Odyssey*, one of our very first books, Telemachus tells his mother Penelope to shut up, but insisting on women's silence arguably predates this intercession: I think men are terrified of women's anger because it hearkens back to our Hall of Fame goddesses, like Kali, who wears a string of skulls around her neck; Medusa, with her halo of snakes; Pele, with the power to burn it all down; and the Furies. It's a long list.

As therapist Harriet Lerner wrote in the 1987 classic *The Dance of Anger*:

The direct expression of anger, especially at men, makes us unladylike, unfeminine, unmaternal, sexually unattractive, or, more recently, "strident." Even our language condemns such women as "shrews," "witches," "bitches," "hags," "nags," "man-haters," and "castrators." They are unloving and unlovable. They are devoid of femininity. . . . It is an interesting sidelight that our language—created and codified by men—does not have *one* unflattering term to describe men who vent their anger at women. Even such epithets as "bastard" and "son of a bitch" do not condemn the man but place the blame on a woman—his mother!

Forty years on, this still sounds about right.

Anger is rooted in boundary violations, that part of the soul that says: *Don't tread on me,* or, for many of us, *Don't tread on people who are not capable of protecting themselves.* This assertion of *No more,* or that something must change, is terrifying for many of us to put forth: After all, we are risking relationship loss, both in choosing to change ourselves and in asking that our partners or friends or colleagues change with us. There's a reason that anger scares the shit out of us. (Don't worry, we'll get to a swearing practice later in the process.)

When healthy, our anger can be righteous and world-changing: It's the insistence that the status quo is unacceptable and that we will not tolerate the situation as it is anymore. We would be lost without this current of energy in the world when it points out where our collective systems need to evolve, shift, and expand, and when it insists that there's a better and truer way forward.

And sometimes our anger is unhealthy, specifically when it is rooted in victimization, finger-pointing, and blame—this is Tool 4, or the Villain role in the Drama Triangle (page 27). In these moments, we take comfort in off-loading our pain onto other people, insisting that if they, or the world, were different, we would be different too. Don't get us wrong: There are real victims in the world. We're talking about something that's quite different. This is the energy of victimization or victim consciousness, and it is rampant in our culture. While we all like to get blame-y and vent-y every once in a while, occupying this space as the primary way in which you encounter the world is disempowering. It suggests that you have no autonomy, no control, no capacity to author yourself or your experience. I rely on the Drama Triangle now to catch myself when I fall into this pattern or go below the line. It's human to visit, but no place to live.

Psychiatrist Phil Stutz, co-author of *The Tools* and *Coming Alive,* and the subject of the Netflix documentary *Stutz,* calls this "the Maze," which he writes about a lot in *True and False Magic,* a book I helped him write. When we're in the

Maze, we want to get paid, get revenge, and get the apology we seek. We want all wrongs righted. In short, we're obsessed with what he calls "the booby prize of fairness." The problem with the Maze is that it's labyrinthine and we can get stuck there, stewing in our irritation and rage, convinced that we'll never be free until the hurts we've experienced are acknowledged and put right. We might be waiting a long time. A lifetime.

We must build skill with our anger, which is a hard path in a culture where most women are scared to experience their anger at all: For many of us, it shows up as the slow boil of irritation, frustration, and impatience before it bakes itself into a veneer of resentment. Many of us don't know what it feels like to be lit up by a holy fire, to feel at peace with this insistent and penetrating current of energy. Marshall Rosenberg, author of *Nonviolent Communication,* offers a skillful reframe. Instead of expressing our anger directly at our target (say, a spouse who leaves dirty clothing on the floor), you express your anger as a need: *I am angry because I am needing to come home to a calm sanctuary and not a tsunami of dirty underwear and single socks.* This introduces a buffer that gives your target some space in which to respond without feeling directly attacked—and it's good practice to identify the underlying need and then state it. The theory is that if we become more adept with dealing with our anger as it emerges—and less inclined to stuff it into our bodies, where it shows up as pain, disease, and depression—we will become more skilled in moving it through our relationships without burning them all to the ground.

Though frequently primary, anger can also be secondary, masking shame, fear, or grief: The more willing we become to engage with these hard feelings, the less we try to "keep the peace" and the greater our ability to reach the deepest part of our soul. As someone who siphons off the top of my anger without ever letting it come up, I understand this well. My story has been "I'm not an angry person; I'm rational, calm, and collected." As I've worked hard on my anger in the past few years, I've felt parts of myself come back "online," parts that I thought I lost as I grew up and transitioned from an outspoken and precocious teenage girl to a woman more concerned with preserving people's experience of her as a "nice person." I had become as good as anyone at concealing my displeasure, my frustration, and my rage.

At a retreat recently, I felt angry for no discernible reason. There was no provoking person or event. It was disconcerting, but I recognized that it was important I let my anger stay, that I spend a few days in discomfort reacquainting myself with this core and essential energy. I knew it was important, for one, because when it first emerged, I tried to will or "higher-mind" it away, and I started to feel so nauseous I had to lie down on the ground. It's not much of a revelation, but I felt this in every part of myself: *When you don't express your anger, it will make you sick.* It was only after I recognized what was happening that the nausea passed and I was able to climb back into my chair. Anger is a powerful teacher if we care to listen—particularly when it's an animating emotion or vibrancy that has no clear target. This is the definition of above-the-line anger, which we'll get into later in this chapter.

On the fourth day of my anger's visit, it released—I felt euphoric but also reconnected, grounded into something vital that I realized I had missed. My anger was back, and it brought with it a deeper connection to my body. I hope it stays—and I hope the following pages reconnect you with yours as well. Too many women sacrifice themselves on the pyre of peacekeeping in order to preserve a relationship status quo: May we learn how to *make* the peace instead; this sometimes requires conflict and hard conversations, but it produces a deeper and more abiding peace that requires no sacrifice of self to uphold.

CORE PROCESS APPLIED TO THE SIN OF ANGER
Tool 1: Is It a Fact or Is It a Story?
Excavating Unconscious Stories

For a full explanation of this tool, see page 10.

First, brainstorm some facts relevant to your relationship to anger and asserting your needs. We've offered some examples below.

FACTS ABOUT ANGER

Elise Example: I flipped off a pedestrian the other day.

Courtney Example: I become angry when my kids leave their towels on the floor.

YOUR FACTS:

1. _____

2. _____

3. _____

Tip: Are these facts capable of being documented by a video recorder? For example, "I flipped off a pedestrian" is a fact. "I think she was drunk or crazy" is a story.

Second, brainstorm the stories that you make up about these facts.

STORIES I MAKE UP ABOUT ANGER

Elise's Fact 1: I flipped off a pedestrian the other day.

Stories Elise makes up about that fact: She was one hundred feet away and jaywalking on a dangerous street—how dare she flip out at me.

I think she was drunk or crazy.

If I had fully stopped I could have caused an accident.

Courtney's Fact 1: I become angry when my kids leave their towels on the floor.

Stories Courtney makes up about that fact: My kids are spoiled. I *never* had to be asked to do my chores when I was a kid. (My mother likely has a different story about my childhood.)

My kids don't listen to or respect my requests. This is the hundredth time I've had to ask them to pick up their towels.

Being a mom is hard and unpleasant.

Fact 1: _____

Stories you make up about that fact: _____

_____

_____

Fact 2: _____

Stories you make up
about that fact: _____

_____

_____

Fact 3: _____

Stories you make up
about that fact: _____

_____

_____

    Third, use the questions below to help you brainstorm some of the additional stories you have about anger.

- What stories do you make up about expressing anger?
- What stories do you make up about women who express their anger?
- What stories do you make up about the anger you feel?
- What stories do you make up about others expressing their anger to you?
- What stories do you make up about the times when you've expressed your anger at other people directly?
- What stories do you make up about when you've felt impatient, irritated, or frustrated?

Elise Examples:

- I only get upset when I have a good reason.
- Angry women scare me—particularly if the anger is expressed at someone else. I feel attacked even if I'm not the target.
- I think I'm too "good" to be angry—I should be able to keep myself under control and I don't want people to think they can get to me.

Courtney Examples:

- I will regret what happens if I fully express my anger.
- If a family member or someone that I work with is angry, I need to do something in response.
- I don't have control over many of the things that make me angry. Therefore, getting worked up is usually a waste of time.

YOUR STORIES:

1. _____

2. _____

3. _____

4. _____

5. _____

Now that you've excavated some of the stories that underlie your relationship to anger, go back through what you've written and star the two or three that drive you the most. Those are the stories that we recommend working with throughout the rest of this chapter.

Tool 2: And Then What?

Tracing the Acting, Sensing, Feeling, and Thinking Loop

For a full description of this tool, see page 13.

Take the first story you want to work with from your starred list. You can repeat this process as many times as you want with different stories.

Story: _____

Step 1: What Actions Do You Take?

When I choose to believe this story, this is how I show up in the world:

My behaviors are: _____

I start to prioritize: _____

My attention goes to: _____

Three specific examples in which I notice this story driving my behavior are:

When I:_____

When I:_____

When I:_____

Step 2: What Sensations Do You Feel?

When I choose to believe this story, I experience the following sensations in my body:

In my forehead, I feel:

Swirling	Fogginess	Buzziness
Spaciousness	Density	Sharpness
Scattered	Throbbing	Stirred up

In the back of my neck, across my shoulders, and in my jaw, I feel:

Tight	Twisted	Pulling
Bunched	Itchy	Burning
Cord-like	Clenched	Steely
Rigid	Blocky	Prickly

Across my high chest and upper throat, I feel:

Heaviness	Constriction	Cut off
Closed in	Numb	Melting
Compressed	Achy	Pierced
Unable to breathe	Flatness	Cold

Around the stomach area, I feel:

Knotted	Fluttering	Butterflies
Nauseous	Braced	Hollow
Churning	Empty	Doubled-over

In other parts of my body, I feel:

Racing heart	Trembling hands	Low-energy
Collapsed	Wiggly	Teary
Expanded	Tingly	Stretched

These tables are adapted from Gay and Katie Hendricks's work on body sensations and intelligence. See www.hendricks.com for further information.

Step 3: What Feelings Do You Have?

When I choose to believe this story, I experience the following emotions:

Anger

LOW	MEDIUM	HIGH
Annoyed	Agitated	Enraged
Bored	Disgusted	Furious
Bothered	Frustrated	Hostile
Dissatisfied	Indignant	Livid
Irritable	Irritated	Outraged
Tense	Resentful	Vengeful

Sadness

LOW	MEDIUM	HIGH
Blue	Discouraged	Agony
Down	Gloomy	Anguished
Lonely	Hopeless	Devastated
Somber	Melancholic	Heartbroken
Solemn	Regretful	Grief-stricken
Unhappy	Sorrowful	Mourning

Fear

LOW	MEDIUM	HIGH
Concerned	Apprehensive	Frightened
Guarded	Edgy	Frozen
Hesitant	Jumpy	Panicked
Reluctant	Nervous	Petrified
Suspicious	Startled	Shocked
Vulnerable	Worried	Terrified

Joy

LOW	MEDIUM	HIGH
Calm	Cheerful	Blissful
Carefree	Excited	Delighted
Content	Graceful	Ecstatic
Lighthearted	Optimistic	Enthusiastic
Peaceful	Proud	Elated
Relaxed	Thankful	Expansive

These tables are excerpted with permission from the Conscious Leadership Group's work on Emotional Range. See www.conscious.is for further information.

Step 4: What Thoughts Come Next?

When I choose to believe this story, the following thoughts arise:

I begin to think that:_____

I judge myself as: _____

I judge others [insert name] as: _____

Tool 3: Why Stories Stick

Identifying the Underlying Fear

For a full description of this tool and the corresponding "Flavors of Fear" chart, see page 22.

Take one of the stories that you excavated in Tool 1 and explored in Tool 2. We're now going to investigate the fear activated by this particular story. You can repeat this exercise with as many stories as you wish.

On pages 249 to 250, we have included examples of this process using our own stories.

Story: _____

When I believe this story and consider the actions, body sensations, emotions, and thinking patterns that it generates, what flavor(s) of fear does it most directly map onto?

- Fight
- Flee
- Freeze
- Fawn
- Faint

Tip: If this exercise feels difficult for you, you might consider standing up, repeating your story aloud a few times, and exaggerating the posture your body takes on as you go into the story.

If I were to disregard this story, what am I afraid might happen?

_____

What am I *really* afraid might happen?

_____

Tip: You may need to ask the question "What am I *really* afraid might happen?" a few times in order to get at the root fear that is activated. There is no wrong answer here, just an intention to understand and be with your own experience a bit more.

Does that fear seem most related to:

- A loss of control?
- A loss of approval?
- A loss of security?

As you sit with what you've learned, see if you'd be willing to acknowledge and accept that there is a part of you that feels scared. The goal is to be with this fear rather than pushing it away.

EXAMPLES:

Elise's Story: I think I'm too "good" to be angry—
I should be able to keep myself under control and don't
want people to think they can get to me.

Fear Flavor: Fight

If I were to disregard this story, what am I afraid might happen?

People would think that I don't have it together.

What am I *really* afraid might happen?

I would experience myself as irrational and emotional, unable to deal with life, unable to control myself, and totally unstable.

This fear is most related to: Control

> **Courtney's Story: If a family member or someone that I work with is angry, I need to do something in response.**

Fear Flavor: Fawn and Flee

If I were to disregard this story, what am I afraid might happen?

If I don't take action in response to a family member's or work colleague's anger, they're likely to blame me for their anger regardless of the facts.

What am I *really* afraid might happen?

Our relationship is at risk; our relationship will not survive if they stay angry. And I need to stay in relationship with them to prevent bad things from happening.

This fear is most related to: Security

Tool 4: Welcome to the Drama Triangle

Relating to Stories from Victimhood Consciousness

Story: _____

For a comprehensive explanation of the Drama Triangle, see page 27.

Pick a specific situation in which this story shows up in your life (see the specific examples you listed in Tool 2 for the story you're working with).

Rotate through the three positions of the Drama Triangle and answer the following questions with respect to this situation/story.

You can write your answers down in this workbook and/or use this tool as an opportunity to stand up and voice your answers out loud. Either way, this is not the time to be polite. The Victim, Villain, and Hero all see reality through overly simplified and reductionist lenses. When you take on their voices, we encourage you to use raw and simple language. Write or speak plainly. No one else is reading this material. It's here for you and you alone. We even dare you to have fun.

THE VICTIM LENS

How are you hurt, taken advantage of, or burdened?

_____

What do you find yourself worrying about over and over again?

_____

Where do you feel overwhelmed, helpless, or ineffectual?

_____

In what ways do you feel that life is unfair?

_____

THE VILLAIN LENS

Who do you blame, hold responsible, or see as the enemy?

_____

What beliefs do you have 100 percent certainty about?

_____

What/who needs to do something different to fix this situation?

_____

What do you take very seriously?

_____

THE HERO LENS

How do you ensure you are needed?

_____

Where do you take on responsibilities that are not yours?

_____

What are you avoiding or suppressing?

_____

How do you minimize or distract yourself from any discomfort?

_____

Which role in the Drama Triangle feels the most familiar to you?

_____

What are you most afraid of?

_____

What have you not yet fully faced or accepted about this situation?

_____

What truths or feelings have you not yet expressed about this situation?

_____

Tool 5: What Do These Stories Get You?

Owning the Payoffs and Costs of Our Unconscious Stories

Story: _____

Who taught me this story?

_____

What do I gain from believing this story?

_____

In what way does believing this story serve me?

_____

Who do I get to stay close with by believing this story?

How do I keep this story going?

If I didn't believe this story, what would I be doing instead?

What does this story cost me?

If I discard this story, what do I have to risk?

How do I use this story to keep me from devoting my energy to that which makes me feel truly alive?

In order to discard this story, what role, behavior, or way of being do I need to shed and grow out of?

How would my relationship to myself change if I didn't believe this story?

How would my relationship to [insert name] change if I didn't believe this story?

These questions are adapted with permission from the Conscious Leadership Group's work on the Drama Triangle. See www.conscious.is for further information.

Tool 6: Teach the Class

Reclaiming Responsibility and Becoming the Creator

Story: _____

Remember: You're teaching this class at a women's college, and you want these twenty-somethings to buy into the exact same story that you are working with here. Your students need very specific instructions that they can follow to re-create and live by this story in their own lives. **The advice that you offer to your students should be actions, feelings, thoughts, and beliefs that they themselves can choose and have control over.** Really commit! Win that teaching prize!

Answer the questions that follow to help you create a game plan for your students:

What actions do you take or not take to ensure you keep believing this story?

_____

What other stories, beliefs, or thoughts should you have about yourself, others, or the world in order to keep this story going?

_____

What feelings should you repress or conceal so that this story remains the same?

_____

What do you withhold and from whom?

_____

What do you try to control that you actually can't?

_____

What do you need to believe you are right about?

_____

What agreements do you have to make and/or break with yourself or with others?

_____

What matters the most to you?

_____

What do you need to feel afraid of losing?

_____

What other "shoulds" do you need to believe?

_____

Now that you have reflected on the specific ways you have ensured that this particular story remains integral in your life, what are you willing to take responsibility for and do differently?

_____

The "Teach the Class" exercise is excerpted with permission from the Conscious Leadership Group's work on personal responsibility. See www.conscious.is for further information.

Tool 7: Playing with Personas

Inviting All Parts of You to the Table

For a full description of this tool, see page 40.

When you believe the stories you have about anger, what persona shows up and dictates your way of being in the world?

EXAMPLES:

Leaky Boat Lisa: I am impatient, frustrated, and irritated about little things all day long, but I disown my anger about bigger issues.

Repressor Rebecca: What anger? I'm never angry. I pride myself on staying calm at all costs.

Avoidant April: I fear conflict, so I tolerate discomfort, and I'm willing to compromise. A lot.

YOUR PERSONAS:

Name and description: _____

Name and description: _____

GET TO KNOW YOUR PERSONA

Once you have a name for the persona who shows up when you believe your stories about anger, answer the following questions:

In what situations does this persona tend to show up?

_____

What are some classic phrases this persona often says or thinks?

_____

What behaviors and actions are typical for this persona?

_____

Think of a specific situation in which this persona recently showed up, and allow him/her to directly answer the following questions:

What is the most important thing to you?

_____

How do you make [insert your own name]'s life better?

_____

When did you first make your appearance?

_____

Who did you learn your style from?

_____

What are you most afraid of?

_____

What do you most want?

_____

These questions are excerpted with permission from _Centering and the Art of Intimacy Handbook,_ by Gay and Katie Hendricks. See www.hendricks.com for further information.

THE PAYOFFS AND COSTS OF THIS PERSONA

When I adopt this persona,

I don't have to feel:

_____

I get to be right and make _____ wrong.

I get to control:

_____

I get to avoid:

_____

I get to feel safe by:

_____

But **when I adopt this persona,**

I don't get to try out:

_____

I don't get to enjoy:

_____

I lose the opportunity to:

_____

I lose this aspect of my humanity:

These questions are adapted with permission from *Centering and the Art of Intimacy Handbook,* by Gay and Katie Hendricks. See www.hendricks.com for further information.

Expansion Moves for the Sin of Anger

If you could wipe out the influences of your family, culture, and past and instead approach your relationship to your anger with fresh eyes, how would you act? What would you do and what would you believe? These expansion moves are designed to help you hit refresh and explore with curiosity and openness what you actually want your relationship to your needs and boundaries to be. For more on these expansion moves, see page 44.

Expansion Move 1: Distinguishing Between Anger That Is Above or Below the Line

Many of us feel threatened by anger—both our own and the anger of others—because we have been witness to its unhealthy expression and consequences in our past. When we explore the "sin" of anger, one key distinction we want to offer is anger that is from below the line versus anger that is above the line.

Anger that comes from below the line is anger masking fear, sadness, or shame. Below-the-line anger typically arises when we experience the fear response of Fight. When we are experiencing below-the-line anger, we typically take on the language, attitude, and posture of the Villain in the Drama Triangle. We blame others or ourselves for a problem. We feel attached to our stories and ways of seeing the world. We seek to defend our position, and we attempt to convince others of how right we are. In the body, below-the-line anger causes us to harden and pull away from others. We feel rigid and contracted. When we're experiencing below-the-line anger and are using various tools to attempt to express it, we typically do not experience a release. Rather, the more we express below-the-line anger, the angrier we feel and the more certain we are in believing our stories to be true.

In contrast, when anger comes from above the line, its expression feels like an energetic release. We simultaneously feel more empowered within ourselves yet also more connected and open to others. The expression of above-the-line anger can feel clean and clarifying, like a gust of wind moving out bullshit and allowing for a fresh start. Above-the-line anger says "Stop," or "No," or "I don't like this," while below-the-line anger communicates "You've fucked up," or "What's wrong with you?," or "I'm scared something bad will happen if you don't get with my agenda."

It's important to notice whether we're above or below the line with respect to our anger because this distinction points to the appropriate next step. If you're feeling above-the-line anger, then many of the practices described in this section will help you feel more enlivened, engaged, aligned with your values, and confident in your ability to take care of yourself. If your anger is masking fear, sadness, or shame, then the practices described in this section will have limited utility. Rather, your below-the-line anger then serves as a clue pointing toward a deeper emotion or story that you need to explore.

It may take some time and practice to discern what kind of anger you're experiencing. If you find yourself blaming people or otherwise expressing reactive, fear-based anger toward others, it's a good idea to take responsibility for your actions and communicate what is going on underneath. For example, I recently needed to acknowledge to my ten-year-old daughter that the anger that I felt and expressed when she forgot to apply sunscreen and came home sunburned was me feeling scared about her experiencing pain and discomfort, as well as catastrophizing what might happen to her skin in the long term.

When you find yourself experiencing anger, you can ask yourself the following questions to discern whether it's below-the-line anger masking fear, sadness, or shame or true, clean anger coming from above the line:

- Am I exhibiting some of the behaviors and characteristics found in the Fight flavor of fear (see page 24), or do I instead feel energy rising within me that is not directed toward one person? Do I feel the need to attack or fight with someone, or do I instead feel the need to call out "Cut scene!" to all parties involved?
- Am I using the language of the Drama Triangle (see page 27) and blaming

others or myself for a problem, or can I access humor, lightness, appreciation, and curiosity even as I also feel angry?

- Do I feel strong and empowered because I know what's right, or do I feel strong and empowered because I know what I can control, change, and take responsibility for?
- Even as I feel anger, does my heart feel contracted and closed or open and available?
- As I work through the exercises in this chapter, is the feeling of anger intensifying within me and am I doubling down on my stories and believing them even more? Or do I feel the anger moving through me and do I feel calm and clear about what is mine to do and the next step I want to take?
- Am I willing to feel any sadness, grief, disappointment, loss, or pain that may arise if the situation that I am angry about continues?

Expansion Move 2: Anger Containers, aka How to Express Anger Skillfully

Many of us are holding in old anger—anger from childhoods when we were admonished that "good" girls don't fight and yell, or times when we were coached to swallow, deny, and suppress our feelings of frustration, irritation, and rage. Many of us were precluded from using our anger to stand up and protect ourselves from situations and incidents we didn't like. And many of us have now developed reflexive habits for shutting down and ignoring the cues of anger rather than facilitating its expression and release.

It can be helpful and healing to create deliberate and proactive Anger Containers where you can safely come back into contact with what anger feels like as it is arising in the body and find healthy vehicles for its expression. Remember that above-the-line anger feels like a rising wave of energy in the body, unattached to any particular story: Its healthy expression is not about ranting or launching into a diatribe but rather about the body matching and moving that energy.

Here are some ways that we like to use and express our anger, all of which are designed to exaggerate and move the emotion through the body. While any of these practices can be used in response to anger arising in the moment, we also recommend regularly and proactively using them to flush out old angers that can't be named and to keep your anger pipeline running clean. Any of the ideas we outline below can be done in the company of willing family members and friends or, if you prefer, alone. If you ask friends or family to witness your anger, the key is to emphasize that the anger is not directed toward them. They're there to serve as a witness, not a punching bag.

Animal Kingdom: Courtney likes to *growl* like a dog. It's true. When something happens that annoys or irritates her, she growls. Immediately. Her family knows what is going on, and they also know that no response is needed or requested. This is how she signals her displeasure, and then everybody moves on. Elise doesn't like to growl, but she uses an "S" breath, which she learned from Anne Emerson, a healer in Sedona. She makes her eyes wide, extends her hands, and spits through her teeth like a snake. She animates this move repeatedly—typically in private—until the emotion has moved.

John McEnroe: If set up intentionally, competitive friendly sports and games can serve as effective opportunities to express anger. Courtney here. I play pickle-ball as often as I can, and I sometimes use the game as an opportunity to re-lease anger, such as howling or stamping my feet in an exaggerated way when I lose a point. My partner knows what I'm up to and laughs at how I can take the game so seriously and playfully at the same time. I have another good friend who I play cards with, and we use that time together to exaggerate our anger as well.

Toddler Temper Tantrum: Take yourself back to your childhood when you com-pletely lost your shit, whether out of frustration or rage, without an iota of self-consciousness or fear. Children are great at expressing their anger at an intensity that matches their internal experience. They move the emotion quickly and completely, and then they move on. Get on your bed and punch a pillow. Lie on the floor and shriek and kick or hit the floor. Run to the woods or go to the ocean to yell into the void. Take a shower and scream until you cry. Play some angry music and sing in the car on your way home from work. Find a rage room in your city where you can go to break dishes.

Expansion Move 3: Curse Like a Pirate

There's a reason many comedians like to use the word *fuck* in their stand-up routines. We often experience a feeling of release and of being understood when we invoke swearing to express our anger. Swearing is one of the best tools humans have for expressing the enormity and truth of a situation.

However, there is an art to swearing effectively. As educator and facilitator Sarah Peyton teaches in her workshops and writes in her *Your Resonant Self* workbook, the best obscenities combine a body part with a word to express holiness. Examples include:

- Sweet Mary's tits
- Holy fuck
- Sainted butthole
- Blessed twat
- Sacred shit
- Angelic ballsack

Feel free to add your own. The possibilities are endless.

When you find yourself angry about a particular situation or issue, rather than blaming others or ranting and doubling down on your story or version of the events, just name the situation and then say, "And this is how I feel about it. [Insert obscenity.]"

The key in this practice is not to direct the swearing toward any person. Swearing, particularly using a combination of swear words like those listed above, is a tool to express the magnitude and depth of your emotion. Effective swearing *is not* name-calling.

Just like other above-the-line practices for releasing anger, you will know that you've nailed this practice when you start to feel lighter, clearer, and more connected to yourself and to others. If you find that the swearing is causing you to feel even angrier, that's a clue that there is another emotion or thought lying underneath the anger that needs to be explored.

Expansion Move 4: The Wisdom of Anger

Anger shows us our boundaries—and clarifies where a need is not being met, even if that need might not be immediately obvious. The wisdom of anger is that it points to what needs to move or shift, in part because when we get angry about something, it clarifies what matters to us. Thinking about your irritations, frustrations, and pockets of rage, can you identify what your anger is trying to communicate to you? Can you identify the underlying need or boundary that your anger is asking you to stand for? When you notice yourself becoming irritated, impatient, annoyed, frustrated, or angry, move the emotion through your body and then notice if you would be willing to trust that the anger is signaling something that you care about. Use the Marshall Rosenberg reframe of anger from *Nonviolent Communication* as many times as necessary to identify your values, priorities, and needs. When doing this practice, the key is to keep restating your need until it becomes something that you can provide for yourself rather than something that someone needs to do for you. For example, "I am angry because I am needing you to do your part in household chores" becomes "I am angry because I am needing our home to be clean" becomes "I am angry because I need space for peace and respite." You cannot control whether someone performs household chores. You can control and take responsibility for whether you have space for peace and respite.

I am angry because I am needing:

_____

I am angry because I am needing:

_____

I am angry because I am needing:

_____

Expansion Move 5: Resentment-Backtracking

Resentment is a particular flavor of anger that is often directed at another person when its real gift is intended for us. We typically feel resentful toward another person when they fail to conduct themselves in a way that we had expected or hoped for. However, just as envy often points to an unexpressed want or desire, resentment can often point to a failure on our part to make clear requests and to create explicit agreements. We often feel resentful toward someone because we've performed a particular activity or task with an unconscious expectation of reciprocity. Many of us feel afraid to express our true wants for fear of conflict or rejection. Instead, we secretly and often unconsciously hope that if we act in a certain way, others will remember and do the same. Resentment then arises when the other person fails to hold up their end of the bargain that we unconsciously negotiated in our mind. When resentment arises, it creates an opportunity for us to examine where we feel too scared to ask for what we really want. Resentment also asks us to take responsibility for the times in life when we've performed certain tasks or said yes to certain activities, not because they're things we actually want to do but because we are hoping for something in return.

Expansion Move 6: Find Anger in Your Body

If you have chronic back pain—or any other recurrent issue in your body—it's possible that you've heard of the pioneering work of Dr. John Sarno, an NYU physician who came to believe that somatized emotions, particularly anger, could result in a cascade of pain signals in the brain. He called this TMS (tension myositis syndrome). After doing a comprehensive physical exam to rule out underlying issues,[*] he would push his patients to contend with everything they had suppressed from their childhoods and otherwise. This was the one antidote: not surgery and not drugs. He authored many bestselling books, such as *Healing Back Pain,* and changed many lives—including those of Howard Stern and Larry David, who are both featured in a documentary about his life and work called *All the*

---

[*] Most of us have underlying issues—it's a function of an asymmetrical and aging body. But ongoing research shows that a vast majority of us don't exhibit any pain and that surgical intervention on things like bulging or slipped discs rarely works. Apparently 30 percent of people in their thirties have bulging discs, and upward of 80 percent in people in their eighties do.

Rage. One of his patients, Nicole Sachs, who was diagnosed with spondylolisthe-sis as a teen and told that she'd never live without pain or have children, not only staged a full recovery but went on to become a psychotherapist and his protégée, taking over the emotional work with patients once they left Sarno's office.

In Sachs's book *Mind Your Body,* she argues that while "the pain is not in your head, the solution is not in your body," and that to contend with the pain, you must first start to empty out the reservoir of repressed feelings. As she writes, "When we don't know how to feel our 'unacceptable' emotional reactions to life (shame, despair, rage, grief, and terror), we are diverted from these challenging feelings by something that our nervous systems deem safer: physical pain and anxiety." Sachs has developed an emotional inventory process called JournalSpeak, in which you start peeling the onion to access your deepest feelings about your-self, your family, and the world; you write daily, for twenty minutes, and then you burn what you give to the page. It's free, it's cathartic, and it's worth trying if you're saddled with chronic pain or anxiety, or are conscious that you're carrying around anger that you're ready to give to the fire. It's worth noting that Ennea-gram Type 9s are particularly susceptible to somatized anger.

Expansion Move 7: End Your Complicity

Take personal responsibility for our cultural judgments of women and their rela-tionship to anger. We are just as much active creators in our culture as anyone else. Make a commitment with your friends to end the practice of gossiping about women who lose their shit in public or express their anger and frustration openly. If you catch yourself judging a woman, whether a celebrity, a stranger, or someone in your circle, for becoming angry, voice the judgment out loud and use it for your own learning purposes.

Expansion Move 8: Build Your
Tolerance for the Anger of Others

Many of us are uncomfortable when others express anger toward us. Rather than sitting with this discomfort, we respond by going on the attack and defending/justifying our actions (the Fight flavor of fear); rushing to accommodate and shift our behavior to make their anger go away (the Fawn flavor of fear); or withdrawing and pulling away from the person (the Flee flavor of fear). We can practice catching our default response to others' anger and shift from seeing anger as a problem that needs to go away to trusting that anger creates opportunities for learning and growth. We can thank others for expressing their anger with us so that we can learn what matters to them. We can let others feel anger without taking it personally or assuming it means we should have done something differently. At the same time, we can draw and keep clear boundaries for the behaviors others use to express their anger toward us.

8

SADNESS

Do you feel like you're in touch with your deepest emotions?

**WHAT YOU'LL RECOVER: ACCESS TO
YOUR FULL HUMANITY AND MOST
PROFOUND FEELINGS OF CARE**

Sadness? you might be asking. I don't remember that from the movie *Seven*. In short, it wasn't in there, and it's not one of the Seven Deadly Sins— though it was on Evagrius Ponticus's original list of Eight Demonic Thoughts. At some point in time, as this fourth-century chapbook made its way through the hands of various desert fathers, sadness disappeared. When Pope Gregory I consecrated the Cardinal Vices in A.D. 590 (and assigned them all to Mary Magdalene, ahem), sadness—described by Ponticus as homesickness and a yearning for loved ones—didn't make the cut. As I postulate in *On Our Best Behavior*, I think this is because sadness is perceived as feminine—weak, whimpering, and unthreatening. What's most interesting to me is that while the Seven Deadly Sins have lodged in the minds of women as a list signaling socially prescribed good and bad behavior for women, sadness—or its denial—seems to mostly affect men. I believe that this is because men are conditioned for power— and it is a weakness to experience and express your feelings. For men, anger becomes the only socially acceptable mask to wear.

In *On Our Best Behavior*, I wrote about men who are severed from their emotional core, including their deep desire to connect, relate, and *care*. Niobe Way, one of legendary developmental psychologist Carol Gilligan's former students, has done for boys what Carol Gilligan has done for girls—and their research has come to overlap in fascinating ways. They had the realization that at a certain part of the acculturation process—for boys, at around age eight, for girls, at around eleven—the word *don't* enters their vocabulary. For girls, this becomes "I don't know." For boys, it's "I don't care." But of course girls do know. And of course boys do care: They are desperate for deep connection. One look at our culture indicates what happens to these lonely boys. Wounded boys become wounding men, and we all pay the price. While depression overindexes in women, the theory is that it's less reported in men because of the stigma and shame. Meanwhile, men make up all the ground statistically when you tabulate deaths from despair, suicidality, and personality disorders. Men struggle under patriarchy as much as women. They may perceptibly benefit from its power structures, but they pay for this privilege with their souls.

Because sadness and its repression and suppression are more of a factor for men than women, Courtney and I discussed at length whether to include sadness in this book at all. After all, our primary goal is to encourage women to pursue wholeness—rather than goodness—and sadness is not much of an impediment to this achievement. But we decided it's still worth addressing, particularly because, to quote Niobe Way, we live in a "boy" culture that extends to us all: Girls and women, in their quest to fit in and succeed, often pick up masculine traits and armor, and this can leave us dislocated from our feelings as well. After all, how many of us have hid in the bathroom to cry at work, deeming it inappropriate and unprofessional to let anyone see our despair? How many of us—through wiping away the first inkling of emotion behind the eyes—have choked down our tears and eventually lost the ability to cry?

This tendency to choke down our tears is supported by a culture that has little tolerance for discomfort or for witnessing other people in pain. We want people to *get over it* already, or we Hero them (see Drama Triangle, page 27) and try to distract them from their grief. It takes a lot of skill and strength to be able to sit in discomfort without rushing into action—even passing someone a tissue can, perversely, be an unhelpful action. We have a lot of stories about women and grief, typically tied to the idea of hysteria (you know, that pesky wandering uterus syndrome)—but the primary one for most of us is that our sadness is not welcome here. Do it in private, if at all.

Sometimes we cover over our grief with anger; sometimes we numb, or self-soothe, to keep it stuffed inside. And sometimes we feel overwhelmed, which is also a perfectly natural response. After all, we've collectively been through a lot—it can be hard not to feel and embody existential dread, particularly in a culture that's drenched in grief and doesn't know how to reach or attend to it.

This is another section where the Drama Triangle (page 27) can be very powerful, because if you're engaged in any form of social justice or activism, it can be hard to stay "above the line," where you feel open, connected, creative, and empowered to act in the world. More often we find ourselves "below the line," where events across the globe are happening to us, whether this is reality or not. When we are "below the line," it can be hard to find a way forward. Hopefully, the following pages will give you some ideas about how to shift the stories you hold.

CORE PROCESS APPLIED TO THE SIN OF SADNESS
Tool 1: Is It a Fact or Is It a Story?
Excavating Unconscious Stories

For a full explanation of this tool, see page 10.

First, brainstorm some facts relevant to your relationship to sadness and deep feelings. We've offered some examples below.

FACTS ABOUT SADNESS

Elise Example: The night our first child was born, my husband cried many times.

Courtney Example: The last time I cried was when a friend of mine died from cancer. She was my age with three teenage children.

YOUR FACTS:

1. _____

2. _____

3. _____

Tip: Are these facts capable of being documented by a video recorder? For example, "Of the 5 percent of the U.S. population diagnosed with depression, 60 percent are women and 40 percent are men" is a fact. "Women have more to be sad and depressed about than men" is a story.

Second, brainstorm the stories that you make up about these facts.

STORIES I MAKE UP ABOUT SADNESS

Elise's Fact 1:

The night our first child was born, my husband cried many times.

Stories Elise makes up about that fact:

I'm glad he cared because he had told me he was worried he would feel nothing and that freaked me out.

I realized I hadn't seen him cry before, so I thought maybe he'd never recover or stop crying.

I believed his emotion that day meant he would be a really good dad.

Courtney's Fact 1:

The last time I cried was when a friend of mine died from cancer. She was my age with three teenage children.

Stories Courtney makes up about that fact:

It's not fair that my friend died this young.

Life is unpredictable and random, and you never know what could happen next.

I can't fully express how sad I feel with others for fear of upsetting them.

Fact 1: _____

Stories you make up about that fact: _____

_____

_____

Fact 2: _____

Stories you make up about that fact: _____

_____

_____

Fact 3: _____

Stories you make up about that fact: _____

_____

_____

Third, use the questions on the next page to help you brainstorm some of the additional stories you have about sadness.

- What stories do you make up about expressing your sadness?
- What stories do you make up about when sadness is appropriate and when it's not?
- What stories do you make up about the sadness you feel?
- What stories do you make up about others expressing their sadness to you?
- What stories do you make up about women who express their sadness?
- What stories do you make up about men who express their sadness?

Elise Examples:

- I can't cry unless I watch a really sad movie—typically about animals. Sometimes I sob for hours because I cry so infrequently.
- I worry that my grief will be totally paralyzing if I tap into it and that I'll feel hopeless about the world. I don't have that luxury.
- Sometimes I find myself comparing traumatic events in the Suffering Olympics—and judging people for having big reactions to things I think they should "get over."

Courtney Examples:

- If I were to fully express all the sadness I feel, I might not be able to get out of bed and function.
- There are certain circumstances when it's more appropriate to express sadness than others. For example, I do everything I can to avoid crying at work.
- I look messy, unattractive, and out of control when I cry.

YOUR STORIES:

1. _____

2. _____

3. _____

4. _____

5. _____

Now that you've excavated some of the stories that underlie your relationship to sadness and deep feeling, go back through what you've written and star the two or three that drive you the most. Those are the stories that we recommend working with throughout the rest of this chapter.

Tool 2: And Then What?
Tracing the Acting, Sensing, Feeling, and Thinking Loop

For a full description of this tool, see page 13.

Take the first story you want to work with from your starred list. You can repeat this process as many times as you want with different stories.

Story: _____

Step 1: What Actions Do You Take?

When I choose to believe this story, this is how I show up in the world:

My behaviors are: _____

I start to prioritize: _____

My attention goes to: _____

Three specific examples in which I notice this story driving my behavior are:

When I:_____

When I:_____

When I:_____

Step 2: What Sensations Do You Feel?

When I choose to believe this story, I experience the following sensations in my body:

In my forehead, I feel:

Swirling	Fogginess	Buzziness
Spaciousness	Density	Sharpness
Scattered	Throbbing	Stirred up

In the back of my neck, across my shoulders, and in my jaw, I feel:

Tight	Twisted	Pulling
Bunched	Itchy	Burning
Cord-like	Clenched	Steely
Rigid	Blocky	Prickly

Across my high chest and upper throat, I feel:

Heaviness	Constriction	Cut off
Closed in	Numb	Melting
Compressed	Achy	Pierced
Unable to breathe	Flatness	Cold

Around the stomach area, I feel:

Knotted	Fluttering	Butterflies
Nauseous	Braced	Hollow
Churning	Empty	Doubled-over

In other parts of my body, I feel:

Racing heart	Trembling hands	Low-energy
Collapsed	Wiggly	Teary
Expanded	Tingly	Stretched

These tables are adapted from Gay and Katie Hendricks's work on body sensations and intelligence. See www.hendricks.com for further information.

Step 3: What Feelings Do You Have?

When I choose to believe this story, I experience the following emotions:

Anger

LOW	MEDIUM	HIGH
Annoyed	Agitated	Enraged
Bored	Disgusted	Furious
Bothered	Frustrated	Hostile
Dissatisfied	Indignant	Livid
Irritable	Irritated	Outraged
Tense	Resentful	Vengeful

Sadness

LOW	MEDIUM	HIGH
Blue	Discouraged	Agony
Down	Gloomy	Anguished
Lonely	Hopeless	Devastated
Somber	Melancholic	Heartbroken
Solemn	Regretful	Grief-stricken
Unhappy	Sorrowful	Mourning

Fear

LOW	MEDIUM	HIGH
Concerned	Apprehensive	Frightened
Guarded	Edgy	Frozen
Hesitant	Jumpy	Panicked
Reluctant	Nervous	Petrified
Suspicious	Startled	Shocked
Vulnerable	Worried	Terrified

Joy

LOW	MEDIUM	HIGH
Calm	Cheerful	Blissful
Carefree	Excited	Delighted
Content	Graceful	Ecstatic
Lighthearted	Optimistic	Enthusiastic
Peaceful	Proud	Elated
Relaxed	Thankful	Expansive

These tables are excerpted with permission from the Conscious Leadership Group's work on emotions. See www.conscious.is for further information.

Step 4: What Thoughts Come Next?

When I choose to believe this story, the following thoughts arise:

I begin to think that:_____

I judge myself as: _____

I judge others [insert name] as: _____

Tool 3: Why Stories Stick

Identifying the Underlying Fear

For a full description of this tool and the corresponding "Flavors of Fear" chart, see page 22.

Take one of the stories that you excavated in Tool 1 and explored in Tool 2. We're now going to investigate the fear activated by this particular story.

You can repeat this exercise for as many stories as you wish.

On page 280, we have included examples of this process using our own stories.

Story: _____

When I believe this story and consider the actions, body sensations, emotions, and thinking patterns that it generates, what flavor(s) of fear does it most directly map onto?

- Fight
- Flee
- Freeze
- Fawn
- Faint

Tip: If this exercise feels difficult for you, you might consider standing up, repeating your story aloud a few times, and exaggerating the posture your body takes on as you go into the story.

If I were to disregard this story, what am I afraid might happen?

_____

What am I *really* afraid might happen?

_____

Tip: You may need to ask the question "What am I *really* afraid might happen?" a few times in order to get at the root fear that is activated. There is no wrong answer here, just an intention to understand and be with your own experience a bit more.

Does that fear seem most related to:

- A loss of control?
- A loss of approval?
- A loss of security?

As you sit with what you've learned, see if you'd be willing to acknowledge and accept that there is a part of you that feels scared. The goal is to be with this fear rather than pushing it away.

EXAMPLES:

> Elise's Story: I worry that my grief will be totally paralyzing if I tap into it and that I'll feel hopeless about the world. I don't have that luxury.

Fear Flavor: Faint

If I were to disregard this story, what am I afraid might happen?

I wouldn't get out of bed.

What am I *really* afraid might happen?

That my children would see how worried I am about the world and they would worry too—I don't want to pass my existential anxiety on to them and ruin their childhoods. And I don't want them to feel as hopeless as I sometimes do.

This fear is most related to: Security

> Courtney's Story: It's not fair that my friend died this young.

Fear Flavor: Fight and then Faint

If I were to disregard this story, what am I afraid might happen?

I'd have to sit and be with how utterly bereft and sad I am that my friend died. I'd have to sit with the sadness and worry I feel for her family.

What am I *really* afraid might happen?

I would feel hopeless and despairing. I'd have to face that death comes for all of us.

This fear is most related to: Control

Tool 4: Welcome to the Drama Triangle

Relating to Stories from Victimhood Consciousness

Story: _____

For a comprehensive explanation of the Drama Triangle, see page 27.

Pick a specific situation in which this story shows up in your life (see the specific examples you listed in Tool 2 for the story you're working with).

Rotate through the three positions of the Drama Triangle and answer the following questions with respect to this situation/story.

You can write your answers down in this workbook and/or use this tool as an opportunity to stand up and voice your answers out loud. Either way, this is not the time to be polite. The Victim, Villain, and Hero all see reality through overly simplified and reductionist lenses. When you take on their voices, we encourage you to use raw and simple language. Write or speak plainly. No one else is reading this material. It's here for you and you alone. We even dare you to have fun.

THE VICTIM LENS

How are you hurt, taken advantage of, or burdened?

_____

What do you find yourself worrying about over and over again?

_____

Where do you feel overwhelmed, helpless, or ineffectual?

_____

In what ways do you feel that life is unfair?

_____

THE VILLAIN LENS

Who do you blame, hold responsible, or see as the enemy?

_____

What beliefs do you have 100 percent certainty about?

_____

What/who needs to do something different to fix this situation?

_____

What do you take very seriously?

_____

THE HERO LENS

How do you ensure you are needed?

_____

Where do you take on responsibilities that are not yours?

_____

What are you avoiding or suppressing?

_____

How do you minimize or distract yourself from any discomfort?

_____

REFLECTION

Which role in the Drama Triangle feels the most familiar to you?

_____

What are you most afraid of?

_____

What have you not yet fully faced or accepted about this situation?

_____

What truths or feelings have you not yet expressed about this situation?

_____

Tool 5: What Do These Stories Get You?

Owning the Payoffs and Costs of Our Unconscious Stories

Story: _____

Who taught me this story?

_____

What do I gain from believing this story?

_____

In what way does believing this story serve me?

_____

Who do I get to stay close with by believing this story?

_____

How do I keep this story going?

_____

If I didn't believe this story, what would I be doing instead?

_____

What does this story cost me?

_____

If I discard this story, what do I have to risk?

_____

How do I use this story to keep me from devoting my energy to that which makes me feel truly alive?

_____

In order to discard this story, what role, behavior, or way of being do I need to shed and grow out of?

_____

How would my relationship to myself change if I didn't believe this story?

_____

How would my relationship to [insert name] change if I didn't believe this story?

_____

These questions are adapted with permission from the Conscious Leadership Group's work on the Drama Triangle. See www.conscious.is for further information.

Tool 6: Teach the Class

Reclaiming Responsibility and Becoming the Creator

Story: _____

Remember: You're teaching this class at a women's college, and you want these twenty-somethings to buy into the exact same story that you are working with here. Your students need very specific instructions that they can follow to re-create and live by this story in their own lives. **The advice that you offer to your students should be actions, feelings, thoughts, and beliefs that they themselves can choose and have control over.** Really commit! Win that teaching prize!

Answer the questions that follow to help you create a game plan for your students:

What actions do you take or not take to ensure you keep believing this story?

_____

What other stories, beliefs, or thoughts should you have about yourself, others, or the world in order to keep this story going?

_____

What feelings should you repress or conceal so that this story remains the same?

_____

What do you withhold and from whom?

_____

What do you try to control that you actually can't?

_____

What do you need to believe you are right about?

_____

What agreements do you have to make and/or break with yourself or with others?

_____

What matters the most to you?

_____

What do you need to feel afraid of losing?

_____

What other "shoulds" do you need to believe?

_____

Now that you have reflected on the specific ways you have ensured that this particular story remains integral in your life, what are you willing to take responsibility for and do differently?

_____

The "Teach the Class" exercise is excerpted with permission from the Conscious Leadership Group's work on personal responsibility. See www.conscious.is for further information.

Tool 7: Playing with Personas

Inviting All Parts of You to the Table

For a full description of this tool, see page 40.

When you believe the stories you have about sadness, what persona shows up and dictates your way of being in the world?

EXAMPLES:

> **Woe Is Me Wendy:** Everything is terrible and I can't do anything about it. I am drowning in despair.

> **Stoic Susan:** There's too much going on to feel much of anything—Who has that luxury? Plus, I would never want to let "them" see me down.

> **Numbed-Out Nancy:** Don't mind me, I'm over here eating/drinking/power-working through my feelings. Actually, I have no idea what I'm feeling, but this Chardonnay tastes great!

YOUR PERSONAS:

Name and description: _____

Name and description: _____

GET TO KNOW YOUR PERSONA

Once you have a name for the persona who shows up when you believe your stories about sadness, answer the following questions:

In what situations does this persona tend to show up?

_____

What are some classic phrases this persona often says or thinks?

_____

What behaviors and actions are typical for this persona?

_____

Think of a specific situation in which this persona recently showed up, and allow him/her to directly answer the following questions:

What is the most important thing to you?

_____

How do you make [insert your own name]'s life better?

_____

When did you first make your appearance?

_____

Who did you learn your style from?

_____

What are you most afraid of?

_____

What do you most want?

_____

These questions are excerpted with permission from _Centering and the Art of Intimacy Handbook,_ by Gay and Katie Hendricks. See www.hendricks.com for further information.

THE PAYOFFS AND COSTS OF THIS PERSONA

When I adopt this persona,

I don't have to feel:

_____

I get to be right and make _____ wrong.

I get to control:

_____

I get to avoid:

_____

I get to feel safe by:

_____

But when I adopt this persona,

I don't get to try out:

_____

I don't get to enjoy:

I lose the opportunity to:

I lose this aspect of my humanity:

These questions are adapted with permission from *Centering and the Art of Intimacy Handbook,* by Gay and Katie Hendricks. See www.hendricks.com for further information.

Expansion Moves for the Sin of Sadness

If you could wipe out the influences of your family, culture, and past and instead approach your relationship to your sadness and grief with fresh eyes, how would you act? What would you do and what would you believe? These expansion moves are designed to help you hit refresh and explore with curiosity and openness what you actually want your relationship to your deepest feelings to be. For more on these expansion moves, see page 44.

Expansion Move 1: Appreciate the Wisdom of Sadness

All body sensations and emotions have an innate intelligence. When we disentangle ourselves from the stories we have inherited about sadness and instead fully experience the emotion and the body sensations or movements it tends to produce (e.g., tears, constricted throat, sobbing, or curling into the fetal position), a knowing should arise within us. The wisdom of grief is that it is pointing us to someone or something that we are in the process of shedding. The mourning process is about fully letting go of a person, relationship, opportunity, home, period of life, et cetera, and recalibrating our orientation to life in its absence. Stillness, contemplation, and retreating typically accompany the grieving process because we're facing how to make our way through life without the resource of a relationship, identity, or way of being we have come to rely upon. Therefore, when we feel the sensations of sadness arising in our bodies or when we sense that we are pushing away a sensation of sadness, the question becomes "What am I being asked to shed and say goodbye to?" When we confront this question head on, we tune into the intelligence of sadness and begin to trust why the emotion is arising within us. When we trust our emotional experience rather than managing, suppressing, or judging it, it tends to move more quickly and more completely through us.

Expansion Move 2: Catch Your Unconscious Sadness Expiration Date

Our grief-soaked culture is incidentally . . . deeply uncomfortable with grief. We set a timer for people who have experienced loss with the expectation that they should "get over it," and pretty soon. When we feel sad ourselves, various judgments tend to arise. "I feel messy and out of control." "This is too much attention." "There's nothing I can do, so what's the point?"

While it's often not our intent, we send implicit messages to people all the time that their sadness is welcome but only in manageable doses. When we rush to hand a box of tissues to a friend who is crying, this may seem like a nice thing to do—and it is—but it's multilayered as well. The gesture suggests that crying must feel uncomfortable and messy: This often says more about our own response to someone's tears than about their own internal experience.

Grief and sadness trigger within us the realization that there is much in this world we can't control, and this is a bitter pill to swallow. As we'll discuss in subsequent expansion moves, many of us have deeply ingrained habits to keep grief at arm's length. Over time, these habits compromise our ability to be with the experience of grief in ourselves and with others.

When we are with someone who is feeling sad or when we are feeling sad ourselves, one important practice is to catch the part of ourselves that becomes increasingly uncomfortable with the experience. Discomfort typically manifests as a physiological response. The body starts feeling itchy and squirmy; we feel the need to do or say something. When you're in the presence of sadness, this expansion move calls for you to ask, "How and when does my body begin to signal that it's feeling uncomfortable? What body sensations do I experience that interfere with my ability to just be with sadness?" Once you notice that these sensations are arising, rather than letting them dictate your actions, try as a next step just breathing deeply. We recommend that you also move your body to shift the sensations of discomfort rather than needing the sadness itself to go away.

This expansion move is about building your awareness of the body signals that typically arise when an experience of sadness—whether yours or someone else's—is lasting longer than your body can tolerate. Acknowledging and breathing through the sensations of discomfort allows you to consciously expand your capacity to be with sadness without letting those rising sensations dictate your behavior. Over time, you are likely to notice that your "sadness muscle" grows, and you're able to be with sadness in its full expression, whatever intensity, duration, or form it takes.

Expansion Move 3: Identify Your Grief Response— to Over- or Underfunction

This concept, specifically the list on pages 294 to 295, is adapted from the work of therapist Harriet Lerner, who writes about the habit of over- or underfunctioning at length in *The Dance of Fear*. In short, we tend to either over- or underfunction in times of stress, crisis, or acute grief. The tendency to over- or underfunction becomes particularly pronounced when we experience grief in partnership. If you tend to overfunction, it's likely that your partner will underfunction, and vice versa.

Attuning to the behaviors of over- and underfunctioning is helpful for recognizing when we're stuck in a pattern, a pattern that typically aligns with the Drama Triangle. Unsurprisingly, overfunctioners like the Hero role. Underfunctioners like the role of Victim. During times of acute grief, we tend to occupy one of either of these two polarities. The Hero overfunctions as a strategy to distract and distance themselves from the emotion of grief and the sensations of "falling apart." In contrast, the Victim underfunctions because they're not yet ready to fully release, let go of, and move on from their loss. At some level, by underfunctioning, the Victim keeps the person, relationship, home, period of life, et cetera still alive and present in their lives. Over- and underfunctioning can both be seen as strategies to help us deal with the fear that arises when we experience acute grief. The Hero/overfunctioner is scared to fully experience grief, whereas the Victim/underfunctioner is scared to fully accept loss.

Through this lens, the strategies of both over- and underfunctioning are useful and intelligent; they help us titrate the experience of grief and loss to ensure that it doesn't overwhelm our systems. As we discussed in Expansion Move 2, we don't have a lot of practice being with grief in our culture—when something happens in our lives that forces us to reckon with sadness, many of us are not equipped to fully experience the sensations of grief and to accept/face the reality of loss. We intuitively use the activities of over- and underfunctioning to allow ourselves to experience grief and to accept/face the reality of loss at a pace that our bodies, hearts, and minds can handle.

In this expansion move, we ask you to read through the typical behaviors of an over- or underfunctioner and determine which is your go-to strategy. If you tend to overfunction, then you know your growth lies in gradually increasing your willingness to become "undone." If you tend to underfunction, then you know your growth lies in expanding your capacity to accept loss and all of its implications. Whichever strategy you default to, the point of this expansion move is *not* to judge your choice but instead to respect its intelligence while ensuring you're also building the internal capacities you need to fully process your experience. The goal of this expansion move is to make conscious the reasons why we over- and underfunction to ensure that these behaviors do not become habituated, reactive, or calcified. We want to rely upon over- and underfunctioning as tools that help us consciously graduate into the full experience of grief and loss rather than as habits we become stuck in.

Because this expansion move is about discerning when the choice to over- or underfunction in response to grief is no longer serving us, we don't recommend using it in the immediate aftermath of acute grief. Rather, use this practice when you start to find yourself stuck in your default pattern of behavior. When you start experiencing sensations of stagnation, boredom, or compulsion, these are signs it is time to find a different way to attend to your grief. Elise here. As one example, when my beloved brother-in-law Peter died in 2017, I immediately started overfunctioning: I planned the funeral and service, I closed all of Peter's accounts, I cleared out Peter's desk, I went to look for new apartments for my brother Ben. Understandably, Ben was underfunctioning. This did not become an enduring pattern in my relationship with Ben: In time, he was back on his feet and functioning while contending with his huge loss. However, the only problem was that in making myself so "busy," I had managed to sidestep my own deep grief. In time, I had to stop overfunctioning, do my own work, and be willing to fall apart. I've slightly adapted the following signs from Lerner's list in *The Dance of Fear*—she offers a more thorough explanation.

Signs That You Tend to Overfunction

- You are very certain that you know what should be done to respond to a situation and that you know what everyone really needs.
- Sitting back and leaving other people to deal with their problems feels actively painful to you. You can't be expected to do nothing! There's so much you think you could do to help!
- You're that friend everyone calls in an emergency because you are so responsible, reliable, and "on it." Why would they call anyone else?
- Whether you've been asked or not, you are quick with advice—maybe you even take over or insert yourself into the middle of what's unfolding to mediate or problem-solve.
- You'd much rather focus on other people, typically because it's easier to solve their problems than it is to look at and deal with your own.
- You prefer not to engage in conversations about your own struggles and shortcomings. Not only does this feel too vulnerable, but you worry you might be letting the underfunctioner "off the hook" of dealing with their problems.

Signs That You Tend to Underfunction

- You just can't get your shit together—in many areas of your life. This is so entrenched that it is part of your personality: People refer to you as disorganized and often helpless.
- People tend to talk about you a lot, particularly family or close friends: You draw a lot of attention, worry, and concern for your inability to "get it together."

- Competence is not your middle name: You welcome and invite other people into your life to take control and get you back on track, particularly in times of stress. In fact, you wait for it.
- You experience physical symptoms—like back pain—when there's stress in your world.
- You don't want people who are close to you to see how strong and competent you actually are—in part because it means you'd potentially need to change and be more functional. You don't know how you'd relate to people differently if they didn't think they had a role to play in helping you.

Expansion Move 4: Grieve the Loss of What Might Have Been

Professor, researcher, and therapist Pauline Boss coined the term *ambiguous loss* as she was searching for the words to describe the experience of many people in her research: people who didn't fit the typical grief model with typical losses. This became a powerful idea, a way to give meaning and context to a range of experiences that had otherwise not been named or honored: family members of soldiers who had gone MIA or had perished in 9/11 with no remains to be buried; people who had been adopted, had been deported, or had moved far away from their home countries in the time before easy connectivity; people who had "lost" someone to dementia or addiction.

In 2021, Boss also published *The Myth of Closure,* where she explains that there's actually no such thing as closure: People move forward with their lives, but they're never "over" certain losses. Nor should they be. Relationships are the fabric of life—the absence of someone core to your experience doesn't render the relationship null. In recent years, Boss has expanded the container of "ambiguous loss" to include ghosting, whether by friends or loved ones, and any other loss that defies easy categorization.

While Boss has expanded the definition to include various forms of relational loss, we want to expand the notion of loss more broadly and suggest that it's something we experience more often than we recognize. We can experience loss anytime life does not turn out the way we would like and anytime we move from one phase of life to another, even as we might simultaneously welcome the change. Courtney here: I regularly work with women navigating various aspects of motherhood, and this is a path riddled with loss. There is the heartbreaking loss of the death of a child, a stillbirth, or a miscarriage. But there are more subtle losses that we regularly experience. Some of us register loss when we're given the news that we're having a C-section rather than the "natural" birth we imagined. When we elect to stop having more children and fix our family size, many of us grieve the fantasy of the Thanksgiving table surrounded by kids, even as we're confident in our choice. As excited as my husband and I were to welcome our first child, we also had to acknowledge that our time as a tight twosome was coming to an end. Life was not going to be the same. For many, launching kids into the world comes with excitement and a lot of grief.

We're used to associating grief with big changes, but we experience loss in all sorts of ways. The expansion move we're recommending here is not about equating big losses like death and divorce with smaller ones. It is about acknowledging that, from a physiological and emotional perspective, our bodies and hearts don't register that distinction. Often, when we find ourselves playing out repeat patterns of the Drama Triangle or when we get stuck in a particular narrative or role, one move we can make to shift our experience is to ask ourselves whether some sort of loss has occurred that we need to acknowledge or grieve. Nearly all of us have unconscious expectations about what parenting, marriage, a particular career, or life "as a grown-up" was supposed to be like. Life rarely matches those expectations. When we find ourselves caught in a dynamic, particularly one where we find ourselves frequently angry or judgmental, this expansion move invites us to inquire, "Is there some vision, fantasy, or expectation I had about how this situation was supposed to go that I need to acknowledge, accept, and move on from?" Likewise, in times of transition, even welcome ones, it's worthwhile to pause for a moment and ask ourselves, "What phase of life or way of being in the world am I being asked to discard?" The goal of this practice is to catch and acknowledge just how often we're in some process of shedding. Often life calls our bodies and minds forward, but our hearts need a little time to catch up.

Expansion Move 5: Support Others in Their Grief

When those we care about experience hardship, some of us fall back on platitudes ("I'm sorry for your loss"), pretend that we didn't know something hard has happened ("I hadn't heard"), avoid the person ("I think the best thing they need is space"), or avoid speaking of the loss altogether ("I wasn't sure what to say"). Others of us play the role of Hero and default to overfunction mode. As we discussed in Expansion Move 2, many of these behaviors originate in our culture's inability to tolerate the sensations of sadness and the lack of agency/control that grief evokes. Expansion Move 2 is about recognizing the physical cues that tell us when we've reached our "fill" of sadness so that we can show up for ourselves and for others in ways that are actually helpful rather than reactive or avoidant.

But what are the ways to show up that are truly helpful? In Mark Nepo's book about friendship, *You Don't Have to Do It Alone,* he tells the story of a friend whose son passed unexpectedly. A neighbor—someone this friend did not know well—dropped a note in his mailbox that simply said, "I'd love to go on a walk with you and your son someday." What he meant was that the presence of his late son would be welcome on the walk—that they could talk about him without avoidance. They became the best of friends. What the friend struggling with loss needed was not vague reassurances, distance, or problem-solving; what he needed was someone simply to walk alongside him as he grieved and acknowledge that his son was emotionally present if not physically there.

We would all be well served by learning how to support others during times of grief. And support in these circumstances usually means having the bravery to sit in silence while someone is moved, for as long as needed. Hold presence for someone's grief rather than trying to distract or mollify them. Send a note—*always* send the note—to express that you are moved alongside them and that you will be there whenever they need a comforting presence. The more we can model this for each other, the more comfortable we collectively become with hard things.

Here are some scripts to support you in supporting others:

- To borrow from Mark Nepo's friend: "I'd love to go for a walk with you and your late _____ sometime."
- "I can't imagine what you're feeling and wouldn't presume to try, but I can offer that it would be a great privilege to support you in any way that you'd like. Any chance you'd want to go for a walk this weekend?"
- "I'm so sorry to hear about your breakup/job loss/____ crisis. I'd love to take you for dinner or on a walk if you need to process. I promise I'll just listen and you can unload."
- Borrowing a line from Sheryl Sandberg's *Option B,* be time-specific: Instead of "How are you doing?," ask "How are you doing this morning?" This acknowledges that grief is a strange journey and emotions move throughout the day: Saying you're okay to a big, fat, general "How are you doing?" can feel like you're saying you're okay with your loss.

Expansion Move 6: Be Okay with Disappointment

Several of the expansion moves described in this chapter have been about situations when there is acute grief, though we experience sadness and loss much more often than that. The word many of us have come to use as an appropriate stand-in for sadness about the little things is *disappointed*. I'm disappointed you missed my birthday party. I'm disappointed we had an argument. I'm disappointed to not have been given a promotion. I'm disappointed this vacation is ending. I'm disappointed you don't want to do what I want to do. *Disappointed* is the code word grown-ups have learned to say instead of "I feel sad." (Disappointment also serves as a stand-in for when sadness mixes with anger and/or fear, so be on the lookout for a combination of feelings as well.)

Because our culture is uncomfortable with sadness, we have learned to skip over when we feel its twinges. Our lack of comfort, even with using the word *sad,* further distances us from the true recognition of what we're feeling. For those of us who are parents, we have also learned early on that our job is about soothing and making sadness go away. This is appropriate in the early years, when distress signals fatigue, hunger, or a dirty diaper, but it becomes more complicated as children grow and feel sadness in a whole range of circumstances. The expansion move recommended here is to notice when you or others use the word *disap-*

pointed and stop to inquire whether it would be more accurate to say *sad*. (Check for fear and anger as well.) Next, many of us have come to believe that disappointment is a problem, that when someone says they're disappointed, it's our job to somehow make it better. When someone important in your life says they're disappointed, notice within yourselves whatever stories arise in response: "This is my fault." "He/she is blaming me for this." "It's my responsibility to make this go away." These are stories ripe for you to use with the Core Process.

Last, all of us have adapted strategies to navigate when others feel disappointed. We've listed some of the most common ones below (all of which are different expressions of the three roles in the Drama Triangle). Scan the list and see which resonate for you. They are all great capacities to have access to, but this practice is about noticing when you reach for one of these tools out of habit or because you have an assumption that someone else's disappointment is yours to fix. (This is also how the sin of sloth intersects with the sin of sadness. Many of us are overdoing because we are not able to tolerate disappointing others.)

Courtney here. I have an agreement with some of my close friends that, rather than jumping in with one of these default strategies, we say, "It sounds like you're having a hard time/feeling sad. What would be most helpful? A hug, a listening ear, advice, or something else?" Elise learned this as "Would you like consoling, counseling, or cheerleading?"

With this expansion move, notice your reflex either to anticipate and prevent others' disappointment or to respond and try to fix it. Instead, would you be willing to accept that small sadnesses, aka disappointments, are simply part of life? Would you be willing to tolerate others' sadness rather than assuming it requires a response?

Common Strategies to Mitigate Disappointment

- **Fixing:** Attempting to fix the problem; stepping in to do something to change the situation.
- **Advising:** Offering solutions and/or statements about what the other person should do.
- **Self-referencing:** Recounting a similar situation that you encountered where you also felt disappointed.

- **Correcting:** Listening for where this person has misunderstood the intentions/actions of you or others and clarifying.
- **Soothing:** Offering reassurances that the feeling of sadness is temporary and will go away.
- **Rationalizing:** Explaining why whatever happened that is causing this sadness was inevitable.
- **Denying:** Arguing that whatever happened was not that big of a deal.
- **Reframing:** Looking for the bright side or silver lining of the situation and asserting that whatever happened is actually for the best.

Expansion Move 7: End Your Complicity

Take personal responsibility for our cultural judgments of both women and men and their tendency to under- or over-respond to grief. We are just as much active creators in our culture as anyone else. Many of us lament that men don't express their emotions enough, yet we have not done our own work; we have trouble tolerating their sadness without leaping in with one of the strategies listed above. Pay attention to where you may be giving off subtle cues to others that their sadness is not welcome, even as you purport to say the opposite. Notice the physical sensations, emotions, and judgments that arise within you when others are feeling sad and use these reactions for your own learning purposes.

Conclusion: Reclaiming

Stories aren't static "things"—they're emergent and evolving entities that can expand, grow, and move over time. They're frequently beautiful and always interesting, a testament to how we make sense of the world. We are meaning-making machines: Stories weave together to create our identity, though they can disfigure and distort our truth along the way—particularly if they're not ours but are passed down to us via culture and taken in wholesale. We hope we've shown you how we can practically outgrow them, deciding when it's time to discard the snail shell of a too-small story (particularly if it's not *yours*) and when to move into something that fits you better instead. This is an ongoing process: As you resolve or shift your current stories, new ones—and sometimes even older ones—emerge to take their place. The core process is something you can come back to again and again to process what's present and not working for you. If you go back to the beginning of the book, you'll see that for (almost) every tool, Courtney has included key takeaways, which are ways to take concepts like personas and facts versus stories much further in your own lives. We hope these become embodied and lived concepts that you turn to all the time.

Courtney and I love the idea of wholeness because inherently, nothing is excluded and everything belongs, even the parts of ourselves that we disavow or deem to be unsavory. Goodness, on the other hand, suggests a corollary—that some things are "bad," or irredeemable. It feels like a position that must be defended rather than embraced into a whole. The other beautiful quality of wholeness is that while *it* is complete, we are not—life is an ongoing practice of reclaiming and realizing all the various parts of ourselves. It is a process of constant discovery and change. We get stuck only when we are mired in stories and social constructions, ideas that keep us fixed in place. It is our greatest hope that these pages get you moving once again.

In each section of this workbook, our goal is for you to develop your own internally driven, consciously chosen relationship to the fundamental human need that each sin represents. The core process is here to help you excavate, explore, and take responsibility for the inherited stories that you have internalized as your own. The expansion moves are here to support experimentation with new ways of being so that you develop a fresh relationship with the sin and what it represents. In the realm of sloth, for example, whether you continue to work sixty hours a week, quit your job, rip up your to-do list, or maybe start going to bed an hour earlier, those choices are yours. We couldn't possibly come up with what your relationship to rest, work, and play *should* look like because the point is that these decisions are yours to make. We want to support you in the quest to rediscover your inner compass, and we want all of us to make decisions about work, rest, and play, not from a place of good/bad or right/wrong but from a place of what feels internally resonant, aligned, and essentially whole. Ditto for every other chapter.

This final exercise is designed to be a temperature check on your current relationship to the sins. Based on your aspirations, desires, and learnings to date, what do *you* want your relationship to each of these sins to be? With those desires in mind, what steps are you willing to take? We want you to live the life you want.

SLOTH

With respect to my relationship to work, rest, and play:

What do I want?

_____

What do I really want?

_____

What do I really, really want?

_____

What is the simplest action I can commit to taking in service of what I want?

_____

ENVY

With respect to my relationship to my wanting, ambition, and desire:

What do I want?

_____

What do I really want?

_____

What do I really, really want?

_____

What is the simplest action I can commit to taking in service of what I want?

_____

PRIDE

With respect to my relationship to the expression of my gifts, and appreciation, affirmation, and praise:

What do I want?

_____

What do I really want?

_____

What do I really, really want?

_____

What is the simplest action I can commit to taking in service of what I want?

_____

GLUTTONY

With respect to my relationship to the expression of my body and experience of pleasure:

What do I want?

_____

What do I really want?

_____

What do I really, really want?

_____

What is the simplest action I can commit to taking in service of what I want?

_____

GREED

With respect to my relationship to money and scarcity and the experience of "enough":

What do I want?

_____

What do I really want?

_____

What do I really, really want?

_____

What is the simplest action I can commit to taking in service of what I want?

_____

LUST

With respect to my relationship to the expression of my sexuality, its pleasure, and its creative potential:

What do I want?

_____

What do I really want?

_____

What do I really, really want?

_____

What is the simplest action I can commit to taking in service of what I want?

_____

ANGER

With respect to my relationship to anger and its expression of my needs and boundaries:

What do I want?

_____

What do I really want?

_____

What do I really, really want?

_____

What is the simplest action I can commit to taking in service of what I want?

_____

SADNESS

With respect to my relationship to my grief and the full expression of my humanity:

What do I want?

_____

What do I really want?

_____

What do I really, really want?

_____

What is the simplest action I can commit to taking in service of what I want?

_____

STORIES THAT I WANT TO CONTINUE TO WORK ON

1. _____

2. _____

3. _____

4. _____

5. _____

Resources, Books, and Websites Mentioned

You can find additional tutorials on the Core Process—including videos—on choosingwholenessovergoodness.com.

While you can get a taste of Byron Katie's books, cited on the next page, you'll also find a host of additional materials, including worksheets and opportunities to join Zoom sessions on her website (thework.com). Elise interviewed Katie for *The goop Podcast* in an episode called "Ending the War on Self."

Elise has worked with psychic medium and channel Carissa Schumacher for many years. You can find information on Carissa at her website (thespirit transmissions.com), including opportunities to attend journeys. Elise has interviewed Carissa many times on *Pulling the Thread*.

Courtney has studied with and led work with the Conscious Leadership Group (conscious.is) for many years. While they've published a book, cited on the next page, they offer a lot of free materials and worksheets on their website as well.

Anne Emerson (thepassionatejourney.com) is an intuitive and coach who works with limited self-conscious beliefs, which are typically stories not attached to any facts. Elise has written about her work on her Substack (eliseloehnen.substack.com) and has hosted her on *Pulling the Thread*.

Gay and Katie Hendricks lead the Hendricks Institute (hendricks.com), where you can find many resources and worksheets, as well as opportunities to join their workshops. They've also written many books, one of which is listed on the next page. Elise has hosted Katie on *Pulling the Thread* in an episode titled "The Upper Limit Problem."

Courtney first met Holly Grant through their mutual interest in the Conscious Leadership Group. Holly has been a senior executive in the venture and fintech start-up investment space for over a decade. She writes about the culture and system of money that we live in on her Substack, *Meditations on Money* (www.hollyngrant.com).

Lacy Phillips is the co-host of the *To Be Magnetic* podcast and the creator of To Be Magnetic (tobemagnetic.com), which is a process of manifestation that requires addressing limiting beliefs. Elise has hosted Lacy on *Pulling the Thread* in an episode titled "Manifesting What We Actually Want."

Prune Harris (pruneharris.com) is an energy healer and Celtic shaman who teaches self-healing practices to thousands. She offers group work as well as hundreds of free YouTube videos.

John Luckovich (johnluckovich.com) is a personal coach and leading thinker in the Enneagram field. He offers private coaching and teaches workshops and retreats.

Bly, Robert. *A Little Book on the Human Shadow.* New York: HarperOne, 1988.

Boss, Pauline. *The Myth of Closure: Ambiguous Loss in a Time of Pandemic and Change.* New York: W. W. Norton, 2022.

Dethmer, Jim, Diana Chapman, and Kaley Warner Klemp. *The 15 Commitments of Conscious Leadership: A New Paradigm for Sustainable Success.* Self-published, 2014.

Emerald, David. *3 Vital Questions: Transforming Workplace Drama.* Bainbridge Island, Wash.: Polaris Publishing, 2019.

Gilligan, Carol. *In a Different Voice: Psychological Theory and Women's Development.* Cambridge, Mass.: Harvard University Press, 1993.

Gilligan, Carol. *In a Human Voice.* Cambridge, Mass.: Polity Press, 2023.

Gordon, James. *Transforming Trauma: The Path to Hope and Healing.* New York: HarperOne, 2021.

Gottlieb, Lori. *Maybe You Should Talk to Someone.* New York: Harper, 2019.

Hendricks, Gay, and Kathlyn Hendricks. *Centering and the Art of Intimacy Handbook: A New Psychology of Close Relationships.* Ojai, Calif.: Hendricks Institute Publishing, 2022.

Johnson, Robert. *Owning Your Own Shadow.* San Francisco: Harper San Francisco, 2009.

Katie, Byron. *Loving What Is: Four Questions That Can Change Your Life.* New York: Harmony, 2002.

Lerner, Harriet. *The Dance of Anger: A Woman's Guide to Changing the Patterns of Intimate Relations.* New York: William Morrow, 2014.

Lerner, Harriet. *The Dance of Fear: Rising Above Anxiety, Fear, and Shame to Be Your Best and Bravest Self.* New York: Perennial Currents, 2005.

Loewentheil, Kara. *Take Back Your Brain: How a Sexist Society Gets in Your Head—and How to Get It Out.* New York: Penguin Life, 2024.

Luckovich, John. *The Instinctual Drives and the Enneagram.* Self-published, 2021.

Nepo, Mark. *You Don't Have to Do It Alone: The Power of Friendship.* New York: St. Martin's Essentials, 2024.

Orenstein, Peggy. *Girls & Sex: Navigating the Complicated New Landscape.* New York: Harper, 2016.

Perel, Esther. *Mating in Captivity: Unlocking Erotic Intelligence.* New York: Harper, 2006.

Peyton, Sarah. *Your Resonant Self Workbook: From Self-Sabotage to Self-Care.* New York: W. W. Norton, 2021.

Rosenberg, Marshall. *Nonviolent Communication: A Language of Life.* Encinitas, Calif.: PuddleDancer, 2015.

Sachs, Nicole. *Mind Your Body: A Revolutionary Program to Release Chronic Pain and Anxiety.* New York: Avery Publishing Group, 2025.

Schwartz, Richard. *No Bad Parts: Healing Trauma and Restoring Wholeness with the Internal Family Systems Model.* Boulder, Colo.: Sounds True, 2021.

Stutz, Phil. *True and False Magic.* With Elise Loehnen. New York: Penguin Random House, 2025.

Twist, Lynne. *The Soul of Money: Transforming Your Relationship with Money and Life.* With Teresa Barker. 2003. Reprint, New York: W. W. Norton, 2017.

van der Kolk, Bessel. *The Body Keeps the Score: Brain, Mind, and Body in the Healing of Trauma.* New York: Penguin Books, 2015.

Way, Niobe. *Rebels with a Cause: Reimagining Boys, Ourselves, and Our Culture.* New York: Dutton, 2024.

Weller, Francis. *The Wild Edge of Sorrow: Rituals of Renewal and the Sacred Work of Grief.* Berkeley, Calif.: North Atlantic Books, 2015.

Acknowledgments

Thank you to the women of Boone, North Carolina, for sparking this core process—and for showing up with such bravery, vulnerability, and grace.

We're immensely grateful to our respective teachers along the way—many of whom are named in this workbook—for guiding our own journeys and for encouraging us to offer our own teachings. We would be lost without our families and friends, as they inspire and hold us accountable to practice the work that we share and teach.

Thank you to all the Jennifers, for bringing us together. And to the Dial Press team: Whit Frick, for letting us go way beyond the remit and meeting us there; Talia Cieslinski, for keeping the project on the rails; Sandra Sjursen, Robert Siek, and Rebecca Berlant for making it real, concrete, and free of typos; Jo Anne Metsch, Aarushi Menon, and Donna Cheng for making it beautiful; and Michelle Jasmine and Debbie Aroff for helping us bring it into the world.

ABOUT THE AUTHORS

Elise Loehnen is the host of *Pulling the Thread,* the author of the *New York Times* bestseller *On Our Best Behavior,* and co-author of *True and False Magic: A Tools Workbook* with Phil Stutz. She has co-written thirteen books, five of which were *New York Times* bestsellers. She was the chief content officer of goop and co-hosted *The goop Podcast* and *The goop Lab* on Netflix. Previously, she was the editorial projects director of *Condé Nast Traveler.* Loehnen lives in Los Angeles with her husband and two sons.

Courtney Smith is a sought-after coach and consultant who works with Fortune 500 executives and other high-profile individuals to achieve change. She is an expert practitioner of the Enneagram personality system, and she teaches the system and other self-transforming tools through workshops and retreats offered to a wide range of audiences. With a JD from Yale Law School, Smith began her career at McKinsey & Co. and then worked as a strategy consultant in the fields of media and public health before becoming an executive coach. She lives in Santa Barbara with her husband and three children.

ABOUT THE TYPE

This book was set in Bembo, a typeface based on an old-style Roman face that was used for Cardinal Pietro Bembo's tract *De Aetna* in 1495. Bembo was cut by Francesco Griffo (1450–1518) in the early sixteenth century for Italian Renaissance printer and publisher Aldus Manutius (1449–1515). The Lanston Monotype Company of Philadelphia brought the well-proportioned letterforms of Bembo to the United States in the 1930s.